Student Congress
&
Lincoln-Douglas
Debate

Second Edition

Student Congress

&

Lincoln-Douglas
Debate

David Mezzera
John Giertz

National Textbook Company
NTC a division of *NTC Publishing Group* • Lincolnwood, Illinois USA

The authors wish to acknowledge Maridell Fryar and David A. Thomas, authors of the first edition of this text, for their many contributions to student congress and Lincoln-Douglas debate.

About the Authors

David Mezzera is currently Director of Community Services at St. Ignatius College Preparatory in San Francisco. While he was forensics director at St. Ignatius, his students won numerous Superior and Outstanding Member awards at the NFL National Student Congress. His team also won the National Championship Congress Sweepstakes.

John Giertz is Director of Forensics at Bakersfield College in California. As forensics coach at Cardinal Newman High School, he has sent numerous students to state-level competition in debate, student congress, and independent events.

1991 Printing

Copyright © 1989, 1981 by National Textbook Company,
a division of NTC Publishing Group, 4255 West Touhy Avenue
Lincolnwood (Chicago), Illinois 60646-1975 U.S.A.
Manufactured in the United States of America.
Library of Congress Catalog Number: 88-60942

1 2 3 4 5 6 7 8 9 0 VP 9 8 7 6 5 4 3

Contents

Part One Student Congress: Deliberative Decision Making 3

Chapter 1 The Nature and Purpose of Student Congress 5

Chapter 2 Student Congress Procedures 9

Chapter 3 The Mechanics of Student Congress 19

Chapter 4 Responsibilities of Student Congress Officials 27

Chapter 5 Preparation for Student Congress 33

Chapter 6 Strategies for Success in Student Congress 43

Part Two Lincoln-Douglas Debate: Confronting Value Decisions 51

Chapter 7 The Structure of Lincoln-Douglas Debate 53

Chapter 8 Debating Value Propositions 57

Chapter 9 The Affirmative Position in Lincoln-Douglas Debate 65

Chapter 10 The Negative Position in Lincoln-Douglas Debate 71

Chapter 11 Evidence in Lincoln-Douglas Debate 77

Chapter 12 Strategies for Success in Lincoln-Douglas Debate 81

Part One

Student Congress

Deliberative Decision Making

The democratic tradition values the individual. It is built on the importance of collective action by informed individuals. Individuals often collectively solve problems they could not deal with alone. In our society, when we wish to enact policy for the larger group, we have chosen to do so through representatives in legislative groups. Student congress is an event that gives to you, the forensic student, an opportunity to work, speak, and function in that deliberative decision-making environment. This section is designed to introduce you to the principles, structures, and organization of student congress. Further, you will be shown how to prepare for student congress and how to utilize some strategies for success in that activity.

Chapter 1

The Nature and Purpose of Student Congress

The application of persuasion in the legislative setting differs from any other situation in one major way. Speaking in legislative debate, or in student congress, is done within a structured environment of specific procedural rules known as parliamentary law. These rules or principles evolved out of the experiences of individuals, action groups, and law-making bodies as rules of order to permit groups to work together efficiently and successfully. In a democratic society, the foundation of parliamentary procedure is rooted in three principles: (1) the will of the majority ultimately decides action and policy; (2) the rights of the nonmajority to speak and otherwise participate must always be protected; and (3) the rules exist to serve the organization and are equally applicable to all of the membership. If you wish to persuade in student congress, you must not only invent the argument and find the data to support it, you must also understand parliamentary rules and the application of those rules in the student congress. You must be sensitive to the shifting weight of opinion within the group and be prepared to offset arguments that are given in opposition to your position. Finally, you must develop the skill of disagreeing with ideas without being disagreeable. This activity allows you to extend your skills of extemporaneous speaking, debate, and interpersonal communication.

The Value of Student Congress

A librarian interviewed by one of the authors contended that of all the students who used the school library for research—forensic students or otherwise—the ones most astute, most politically aware, and most knowledgeable about the techniques of research were the student congress competitors. The attributes necessary to be a competent student congress member are attributes necessary to survive in the "real world" of politics, political science, and persuasion. In addition to practicing a variety of public speaking events, from oratory to extemporaneous to impromptu speaking, student congress calls on skills necessary for successful participation in discussions, debates, and parliamentary situations. An added flavor is provided by the fact that student congress mimics real-life legislative assemblies and presents its participants with an insight into some of the issues and problems that actually confront our lawmakers. What better choice for a learning experience and competitive event than student congress?

The Types of Student Congresses

The National Forensic League, a national honorary society that promotes high school speech competition, recognizes three types of student congresses. *Practice congresses* can be held by any school and may be organized in conjunction with a regular speech tournament or as a separate event. Schools that are not affiliated in any way with NFL may attend and participate in such congresses. However, if NFL points are to be awarded to NFL members, a minimum of four schools must attend. Such practice congresses are very important to the training of student congress members, and if they are available to you, you are fortunate. Every NFL District should try to have at least one practice congress during the year. Coaches who wish to host a competitive activity but who feel that they cannot handle a full forensic tournament should certainly consider hosting a practice student congress.

A second type of student congress is held only once each year for the express purpose of sending students to the NFL National Student Congress. Each NFL District may hold a *District Student Congress* and may send as many as two Senators and two Representatives to the National Student Congress if there are at least twelve schools in attendance at the District Congress.

The third type of student congress promoted by NFL is the *NFL National Student Congress*. The student congress was first held in 1937. Although procedural alterations have been made from time to time, the basic format has remained much the same in the intervening years. The National Student Congress, which meets during the National NFL Tournament, is held in high esteem by students and coaches alike. With over 250 participants each year at the National Congress, the contest is organized into five Senates and five Houses. There are special rules for the National Student Congress, but most of them have to do with the awarding of points and the selection of Superior Congress award winners who advance to a final bicameral session. The legislative deliberation in any of these types of student congress is essentially the same. Specific NFL rules are printed in the form of two booklets entitled *Preparing for Student Congress* and *Student Congress Manual*. Both are published by the National Forensic League and are available from the NFL National Office in Ripon, Wisconsin.

Besides the National Forensic League, a number of other organizations sponsor congressional events. Many of these are parliamentary procedure events. Others are geared to teach the principles of citizenship and government through direct practice. To participate in most of these activities, a student must apply for acceptance. However, some are available to any student who is a member of the particular organization. Some of the most notable are the Junior Statesmen of America, Youth-in-Government (sponsored by the YMCA), state activity league congresses, and Boys State and Girls State, which are sponsored by the American Legion. Students who are chosen to participate in these latter programs organize their own city, county, and state governments. They choose their own officials and introduce and argue their own bills in the legislature.

The 4-H Clubs of America, the Future Farmers of America, and other clubs that emphasize a knowledge of parliamentary procedure have competitive events that make use of teams trained in parliamentary procedure. In addition, their national conventions are organized to give legislative experience to students in attendance.

The types of student congresses in which you may participate and compete are many and varied. However, they all share the common goal of giving experience to students in the use of legislative debate. Because this book is aimed at students who are interested in building skills in the competitive areas, the discussion and examples used here will be drawn primarily from the materials supplied by the National Forensic League and from the experiences of the authors and their students in NFL Student Congress. However, all student congress events have things in common. If you are involved in other groups besides NFL, you can apply the basic principles discussed here within the framework of rules and regulations specified by other groups.

Student Congress Hints

You are now well on your way to becoming an informed member of a student congress assembly. There are only three goals you need to achieve in order to become a proficient and effective participant: Prepare better on each bill (on one or both sides) than other members do, know how to prepare briefs correctly and how to use them in your debating, and know the Table of Most Frequently Used Parliamentary Motions and how to use it better than even the Presiding Officer does! Are you up to the task? Each of these three key elements of superior congress participation will be covered in-depth in the chapters that follow.

The area that seems to cause the most concern to students at the beginning phase of learning student congress is having to use parliamentary procedure. You need not be clever in using involved motions, but you should know how to put common motions into the proper form and know when to make such motions. You will be provided with a table of frequently used motions and with suggestions on when and how to make correct motions. If you hope to chair an assembly as its Presiding Officer, then you must have special interest in and understanding of parliamentary procedure and know why and how it is used. You should know how to state a question in correct parliamentary language, how to take a vote properly, which type of votes to use, and how to announce the result and effect of the vote. For this reason you should carefully study the role of the Presiding Officer found in an upcoming chapter. If this commentary about parliamentary procedure frightens you a bit at this point, please don't worry; just remember that the purpose of student congress is to *debate,* not to show off knowledge of parliamentary procedure.

Summary

Student congress offers you a chance to practice most of the skills used in political discussion and public speaking. The National Forensic League promotes a variety of congresses at all levels of competition. As a participant, you will need to be familiar with the mechanics of student congress, including bill preparation and parliamentary procedure.

Chapter 2

Student Congress Procedures

Certain procedural rules have been worked out by the NFL to insure equity in floor debate. Observing these rules will ultimately benefit all members of the student congress. To participate in student congress, you should be familiar with the rules. You should obey them in order to avoid embarrassment during the debate.

Debate

Procedural Rules

All speeches are strictly timed. No speech, including an authorship speech, may be longer than the specified time. The Timekeeper will be instructed to inform the speaker and the Presiding Officer when that limit is reached. No additional time will be given. During a speech, members may ask for recognition and ask the speaker if he or she will yield to a question. Because the time for both the question and the answer are taken from a speaker's allotted time, the speaker may begin the speech by stating that he or she will not yield for questions until the conclusion of the speech. If a speaker specifies this, then the speech is given without interruption. Then questions are answered as time allows at the conclusion of the speaker's remarks. A special rule can be created by an assembly using the motion to suspend the rules. This rule establishes an automatic cross-examination period following every speech. Some assemblies create such a period for authorship speeches only.

The author of a bill or resolution is privileged to speak first. But once the debate has opened, the legislation belongs to the group and not to the author. Thus, it is not necessary to get permission from the author to offer an amendment. Nor is it correct to ask the author what the bill means. A bill means what it says to the assembly. It is not open for interpretation from the author. Nor is the group obligated to interpret the bill in the same way the author intended.

Following the authorship speech, each member who wishes to speak may ask for recognition only if he or she assumes a position that opposes that of the preceding speaker. Observation of this rule accomplishes several things. First, it insures that the debate is truly a debate and not a long series of "me, too" speeches that do not advance the cause of anything but point gathering by members. Second, it insures that both sides will have an equal opportunity to present their position openly and fairly. It also safeguards the Presiding Officer against charges of loading the debate for one side or the other. It further makes sure that a maximum number of issues on each side will be aired.

Because a member's success hinges on getting recognition and being able to speak to the student congress, another set of procedures is enforced. First, Presiding Officers call on speakers in the inverse order of the number of speeches they have delivered—that is, that recognize those who have not spoken or have spoken less often before those who have spoken more frequently. In addition, a member may speak only five times a day. When a member has reached this limit, the Official Scorer will mark his or her name off the seating chart, and he or she may be recognized only if no other member of the assembly wishes to speak. Finally, toward the end of the session, the Presiding Officer may announce that until further notice recognition will go only to those who have not spoken more than once. If, however, debate begins to lag, indicating that those who have not spoken more than once do not desire to do so, the Presiding Officer can return to general recognition.

Etiquette

In addition to the restrictions and limitations placed on the length and substance of floor speeches, you need to be familiar with the etiquette of student congress. There is a right and a wrong way to speak in a legislative session. When referring to another participant, use the terminology "Representative Green" or "the Representative from West Texas." Such terminology helps to keep the entire group aware that their positions, temporarily at least, are ones of dignity and seriousness, and underscores the fact that each competitor is playing the role of a member of a legislative body. The Presiding Officer should always be addressed as "Mr. or Mme. Speaker." If the house has been designated as a Senate, then the term for the Presiding Officer is "Mr. or Mme. President."

The proper way to gain the floor in order to make a motion or to participate in debate is to rise as soon as the preceding speaker has finished and at the same time say, "Mr. President" (or "Mme. Speaker"). If the Presiding Officer recognizes you, he or she will state, "The chair recognizes Representative Green." You may then make your motion or give a speech on the pending legislation. If, however, another member of the assembly is recognized, resume your seat until he or she has finished. To interrupt a speaker for questioning, use the following language: "Mr. Speaker (or Mme. President), will the speaker yield for a question?" The chair will then ask the speaker if he or she wishes to yield. If so, you may then ask one question. If not, you resume your seat and do not interrupt again. The Presiding Officer should discourage frequent interruptions of the same speaker. If the speaker has prefaced his or her remarks by saying he or she will not yield until the speech is finished, then no one will be recognized during the speech.

Under no circumstances are you or any other member of the student congress allowed to argue with the Presiding Officer. He or she has been elected to that position, and his or her decisions are final. The decisions are only discussed if there is a failure to follow parliamentary procedure and a violation of the rights of the assembly. Even then, there are two recourses. First, the Parliamentarian should intervene without any remonstrance from the membership. If this does not occur, however, you may "Rise to a point of order" or "Appeal the decision of the Chair." These should be used only if you have a sound parliamentary reason, not a personal one. (These motions are dealt with in the upcoming Table of Most Frequently Used Parliamentary Motions.)

Parliamentary Procedure

Parliamentary procedure is a useful tool that must be respected and used for the purposes for which it was designed. The basic principles of parliamentary law, once understood and accepted, make its many rules easy to understand. Parliamentary rules, first and foremost, exist to make it easier to transact business. They exist to promote cooperation, not to create disharmony. All groups that operate under parliamentary laws are dedicated to the precept that the majority will decide the action of the group. But they are also equally committed to the concept that all members have rights and privileges that must be safeguarded. Furthermore, particularly in a legislative assembly, parliamentary rules are intended to insure that full and free debate of every proposition will be allowed. Parliamentary law is built on the idea that time and effort should be utilized and that decisions should be reached by the simplest and most direct procedure. Specific rules of parliamentary procedure allow for a definite and logical order or priority for business. They also insure that every member has the right at all times to know what is being done by the assembly. These basic concepts of democratic procedure are accomplished by the judicious and fair application of parliamentary procedure. The most important thing for you to remember is that the ultimate purpose of parliamentary procedure is to insure the rule of the majority and to guard the rights of the minority. Used properly, it will keep debate going and will allow for full discussion. The Parliamentarian, the Presiding Officer, and each individual member should be dedicated to this principle and should strive to guarantee its fulfillment in the student congress.

It is not necessary to be a "parliamentary card shark." In fact, if you attempt to use the floor of student congress to show off long and involved or clever motions, you will be quickly spotted as an obstructionist and will have difficulty getting the floor thereafter. As stated earlier, the purpose of the student congress is to debate, not to show off expertise in parliamentary procedure. A good working knowledge of parliamentary procedure allows freedom of debate and gives you the assurance that the proper language is employed.

A motion is a proposal or a suggestion made by a member of a group that he or she wishes the entire group to consider and ultimately adopt. Most motions require a Second, or a second person who feels that the motion is worth discussing and considering. The proper form for common motions is "I move that. . ." rather than "I make a motion to. . ." You should have a careful enough knowledge of the chart of precedence that you will not introduce motions that are out of order. Simply stated, if the motion you wish to present in order to accomplish your purpose is higher on the table of motions than the motion currently being considered, then your motion has a "higher" priority. It is in order at that specific time to introduce the motion to the group for its consideration. If you wish to move with poise and assurance through congressional debate, you will carefully study the parliamentary procedure necessary. In a student congress, certain adaptations of the parliamentary procedure as outlined in *Robert's Rules of Order* have been made. A careful look at the chart reproduced below by permission of NFL will indicate where some of those changes have been made. Notice how the motions are grouped by type into four distinct classes. Try to understand the purpose listed for each of

Table of Most Frequently Used Parliamentary Motions
Adapted for use in NFL Student Congress

Type	Motion	Purpose	Second Required?	Debat- able?	Amend- able?	Required Vote	May Interrupt a Speaker
	24. Fix Time for Reassembling	To arrange time of next meeting	Yes	Yes-T	Yes-T	Majority	Yes
	23. Adjourn	To dismiss the meeting	Yes	No	Yes-T	Majority	No
	22. To Recess	To dismiss the meeting for a specific length of time	Yes	Yes	Yes-T	Majority	No
	21. Rise to a Question of Privilege	To make a personal request during debate	No	No	No	Decision of Chair	Yes
	20. Call for the Orders of the Day	To force consideration of a postponed motion	No	No	No	Decision of Chair	Yes
	19. Appeal a Decision of the Chair	To reverse the decision of the chairman	Yes	No	No	Majority	Yes
	18. Rise to a Point of Order or Parliamentary Procedure	To correct a parliamentary error or ask a question	No	No	No	Decision of Chair	Yes
	17. To call for a Roll Call Vote	To verify a voice vote	Yes	No	No	1/5	No
	16. Object to the Consideration of a Question	To suppress action	No	No	No	2/3	Yes
	15. To Divide a Motion	To consider its parts separately	Yes	No	Yes	Majority	No
	14. Leave to Modify or Withdraw a Motion	To modify or withdraw a motion	No	No	No	Majority	No
	13. To Suspend the Rules	To take action contrary to standing rules	Yes	No	No	2/3	No
	12. To Rescind	To repeal previous action	Yes	Yes	Yes	2/3	No
	11. To Reconsider	To consider a defeated motion again	Yes	Yes	No	Majority	No
	10. To Take from the Table	To consider tabled motion	Yes	No	No	Majority	No
	9. To Lay on the Table	To defer action	Yes	No	No	Majority	No
	8. Previous Question	To force an immediate vote	Yes	No	No	2/3	No
	7. To Limit or Extend Debate	To modify freedom of debate	Yes	Yes	Yes-T	2/3	No
	6. To Postpone to a Certain Time	To defer action	Yes	Yes	Yes	Majority	Yes
	5. To refer to a Committee*	For further study	Yes	Yes	Yes	Majority	Yes
	4. To Amend an Amendment*	To modify an amendment	1/3	Yes	No	Majority	No
	3. To Amend*	To modify a motion	1/3	Yes	Yes	Majority	No
	2. To Postpone Indefinitely	To suppress action	Yes	Yes	No	Majority	No
	1. Main Motion	To introduce business	Yes	Yes	Yes	Majority	No

No. 5 Should Include:		*Nos. 3 and 4 by:
1. How Appointed?		1. Inserting
2. The Number	T-Time	2. Adding
3. Report When?		3. Striking Out
or		4. Substituting
To What Standing Committee		5. Striking Out and Inserting

the 24 commonly used motions and notice the technical information presented about voting requirements for each. You need not memorize such a chart, but you should have a copy handy for easy reference during a congress session.

Voting

Voting procedures serve best when they are carried out in a particular fashion for student congress. For example, voting on legislation and amendments should always be done by a standing vote unless a roll call is demanded by one-fifth of the members. Preference votes and votes requiring a two-thirds majority should be conducted by either a standing vote or a show of hands. At the discretion of the Presiding Officer, some motions may be disposed of by a voice vote; this can be used to simplify and speed proceedings. A division of the house may be demanded by any two members on any question on which such a voice vote was taken. This call for a division to verify a voice vote must be made before another motion is placed on the floor. Votes for Presiding Officers and Superior Members are by secret ballot.

Bills, Resolutions, and Amendments

All business conducted in a student congress, aside from elections, centers around either a bill or a resolution. A bill is an enumeration of specific provisions that, if enacted, will have the force of law. Put more simply, a bill is a proposed law that is intended to solve some problem. Once debated and passed by Congress (and signed by the President), a bill becomes a new law. A bill must be definite and must state exactly what is to be done or what is to be discontinued. There must be some enforcement procedure included in it, and it should specify some form of implementation. Specific items, such as a phase-in time and financing, may be a part of the bill. A penalty should be stipulated if appropriate, or the law will not have any force.

A resolution, on the other hand, is usually a generalized statement expressing the belief of the group. A resolution is, in other words, a proposition of value or fact. The resolution does not carry the force of law. It may be preceded by "whereas clauses" that state the principal reasons for adopting the resolution, although such clauses are not mandatory. A clear understanding of the differences in the form and substance of bills and resolutions is important. Participation in most student congress events is predicated on your submitting either a bill or a resolution and the thrust of the debate could differ depending on whether a new policy or a value judgment is being debated. A resolution will generally center the debate on the broad principles of the concept; a bill is more likely to focus the debate on the merits of the specific provisions it contains.

As you begin preparing to write your own bill or resolution, you need to start either with a problem area that the U.S. Congress might attempt to solve by proposing a new law or with a condition that the group sentiment feels needs to be addressed within a resolution. Consider some of the following types of problems that face our country: military, energy, foreign trade, legal and judicial affairs, education, economy, welfare, crime, national security, and technology. As you finalize your choice of topic, remember that your sentiment or proposed solution must be debatable. That is, it must have two sides to it, a pro and a con, or it will not serve the purpose of an item for legislative debate. It must have information available on both sides, and it should be timely and of current interest.

Both the form and substance of these documents are important. NFL has particular rules concerning the form of a bill and of a resolution. Other groups may have different rules, but those from NFL are useful as a model:

1. The bill or resolution must be typed.

2. The typing must be double spaced, and the bill or resolution may not be longer than one page.

3. The first words of a bill are "Be It Enacted. . . ." Following any whereas clauses, the first words of a resolution are "Be It Resolved. . . ."

4. Each line of a bill or resolution must be numbered.

5. A resolution may be preceded by one or more whereas clauses but bills and joint resolutions (bills introduced into both houses of the legislature at about the same time, such as to amend the Constitution) never have them.

6. The language of a bill must always be in the imperative mood. That is, it must state exactly what is to be done by whom.

The following examples highlight the difference in style and format between a bill and a resolution and show how a variety of solutions might be
offered when you are dealing with a particular current issue.

Simple Resolution

1.   Whereas, few definitive ethical principles have been
2. promulgated by either the medical or legal professions
3. concerning the subject of human organ transplants and/or
4. artificial organ replacements, and
5.   Whereas, not all patients with organ failures have equal
6. access to organ transplantation, and
7.   Whereas, the selection criteria to determine which patients
8. are suitable candidates for organ transplantation surgery are
9. arbitrary at best and discriminatory at worst, and
10.   Whereas, a disparity exists between the number of patients
11. in need of transplantation surgery and the number of readily
12. available organs, and
13.   Whereas, the investment of time, money, personnel, and
14. facilities for transplant surgery is a grossly inefficient allocation
15. of medical resources, therefore
16.   Be It Resolved by the House of Representatives in Student
17. Congress assembled that it is the sense of this legislative body
18. that the proliferation of human organ transplants and artificial
19. organ replacements cannot be justified.

A Bill

1.   Be It Enacted by the Senate in Student Congress
2. assembled that
3.   Section 1. A human organ donor organization, titled the
4. National Organ Donor Program, shall be established under the
5. auspices of the Federal Department of Health and Human
6. Services and a universal donor card shall be created to replace
7. the widely varied state donor cards.
8.   Section 2. A national educational program shall be
9. instituted using Public Service announcements on radio and
10. television and within the print media, encouraging people to
11. join the National Organ Donor Program. Said educational
12. program will be funded from the approved budget of the
13. Health and Human Services Department.

14.   Section 3. All state Health Departments and appropriate
15. private agencies shall be invited to join this national donor
16. system and "pool" their available organs, thus establishing a
17. national donor bank. All agencies and states that do join said
18. system shall be linked via a central computer system that will
19. keep records of available organs.
20.   Section 4. The current system of financing and maintaining
21. organ banks shall be transferred to the control of the
22. Department of Health and Human Services and organ
23. recipients shall reimburse the national donor bank through
24. regular hospital charges and insurance payments.
25.   Section 5. Establishment of said National Organ Donor
26. Program shall begin immediately upon passage of this bill, and
27. all necessary operational needs shall be completed on or before
28. the beginning of the next fiscal year following ratification of
29. this legislation.

If you read these examples carefully, you can see what bills and resolutions should include. Note the use of very specific language and the inclusion of monetary conditions. When writing a bill, you should be particularly sure of what the law is at the present time. Preparing a bill for student congress is much like preparing an affirmative case. The bill is comparable to an affirmative plan. The authorship speech is similar to the affirmative need. It is an appeal for justification for the bill's passage based on conditions that the bill will correct. If you approach that task without adequate research and knowledge, you will probably get the kind of reception you deserve!

A special class is reserved for constitutional amendments. They are classified as resolutions because they must be submitted to the states after they are passed by Congress. They are, in reality, only a suggestion to the states. However, they must be specific like a bill. A proposed constitutional amendment should indicate the part of the Constitution being changed and should specify the desired outcome of the amendment.

Bills and resolutions introduced on the floor for legislative debate may generate another kind of consideration, the amendment. In student congress, because the delegates have had the bills and resolutions well ahead of time, there are certain kinds of restrictions put on amendment procedures. First of all, an amendment must be submitted in written form. The written amendment must indicate (by line number) the exact portion of the bill that is being changed. It must indicate what method of change is employed, whether by addition, substitution, or deletion. An example of an amendment, properly worded, for the preceding sample bill would be

> I move that the bill under consideration before this house be amended by altering Section 4 as follows: On lines 22 to 24, delete all words following "Health and Human Services" and substitute with the following: "and all ongoing costs for maintaining these banks and for transporting human organs for use in transplant operations shall be borne by the federal government."

In order to submit an amendment, you must first send the amendment in written form to the clerk. Then you must get recognition from the Presiding Officer. No special consideration will be given because you have an amendment to offer. Once you have the recognition of the chair, you should stand and say, "I move to amend the motion by . . ." and then state the amendment exactly as it is in writing. An alternative method would be to say, "Mr. or Mme. Speaker, I have an amendment to offer and would like permission for the clerk to read it." In either event, it is necessary for one-third of the assembly to second the amendment before discussion is in order. This rule is a departure from the rules as promulgated in *Robert's Rules of Order*, but it is used in student congress to insure that an endless stream of amendments is not presented as a delaying tactic, as is sometimes the case in the U.S. Senate. Once the amendment is on the floor, then all debate must relate to the amendment until it is either passed or defeated. At that point, debate resumes on the bill or resolution in either its original or amended form.

Summary

The procedural rules that govern student congress debate are designed to enable all members to participate. Parliamentary procedure is your key to contributing to student congress. By knowing the rules governing voting, and the introduction of bills, resolutions, and amendments, you can be sure that you are moving the business forward effectively.

Chapter 3

The Mechanics of Student Congress

For every student, there is a first-time experience in student congress. Although participation in student congress draws heavily on speech skills acquired in other areas and events, there are many characteristics unique to the student congress event. A complete understanding of the mechanics and structure of student congress will help to insure that the experience is meaningful and successful.

Houses and Apportionment

The student congress is organized to replicate, when possible, the actual legislative bodies of our own nation's government. The number of houses a student congress will have depends on the number of schools and students who participate. Consequently, a student congress may be unicameral, bicameral, or multi-house in its organization. Some local practice congresses have become so popular and so well attended that they are organized with numerous houses, each simulating a group of representatives formed into legislative committees considering a variety of legislation. Some multi-house congresses extend the analogy of the U.S. Congress, being composed of a Senate and a House. Thus, the use of Senator, Representative, or simply Congressmember will be considered as equivalents in this text.

NFL experience has shown that a house with too many members will be unwieldly and will not give enough students the opportunity to participate. By the same token, a house with too few students will not offer sufficient interaction to make the experience worthwhile. Consequently, NFL advises that the optimum membership in a house of a student congress is between 20 and 30.

To govern the number of students participating, the individual NFL District will set a particular apportionment for each chapter in the District Congress. If at least 12 schools are participating, the NFL District

19

may send four members to the National Student Congress and would need a bicameral student congress. The apportionment is usually different for Senate and the House. The NFL District Committee may designate anywhere from one to three senators per chapter. In keeping with the principle exercised in our U.S. Congress, the apportionment of senators would be the same for each NFL chapter, no matter what the size. The House of Representatives, however, is based on population. The population of an NFL chapter is the total number of members and degrees held by that chapter. A typical apportionment might be two senators from each chapter and one member in each house for each thirty members and degrees held by that chapter. Practice congresses and State Activity League Congresses can follow similar guidelines for apportionment. Whatever the formula, the official responsible for it will notify the participating schools prior to the student congress.

When participation in the district or state is large enough, it is a good idea to run a tricameral congress and to designate the house that will not be sending representatives to the National Student Congress as the "Novice House." The Novice House provides students who have not previously participated in student congress with an opportunity to learn and experiment with the event without competition from experienced participants. Some NFL Districts restrict such a house to freshmen and sophomores, and some even eliminate participation by students with debate experience. The idea is to provide a training ground for students and, in effect, to help the quality of future student congress participation.

If the student congress is set up as bicameral, an effort can be made to parallel the actual relationships between the Senate and the House in the U.S. Congress. This can be done by following the suggestions made by NFL. For example, when a bill is passed by one house, it can be sent to the other house with the request that the other house concur. If agreement is not reached, or if amendments are offered and not accepted by the initiating house, then a conference committee can be formed to reach consensus. A report from a conference committee or a report from one house to another shall be privileged, but may not interrupt a speaker. This kind of relationship between the houses helps to insure good debate and keeps student congressmembers aware of the larger group.

Sessions

The length of a legislative session depends on the desires and facilities of the General Director of the student congress. Most practice and district congresses hold a one-day session; many others, such as state-wide or invitational congresses, hold two-day sessions. NFL rules specify that each legislative day of a District or National Congress must contain a minimum of five hours of floor debate in addition to the time used for committee meetings or elections. For a one-day congress, it is possible to have a morning and an afternoon session, each of about three hours' duration. When an agenda, or order of business, for a congress session calls for committee meetings, these may be accomplished either formally or informally. Committees frequently are asked to review proposed bills and resolutions, to choose appropriate legislation for later congresses, or to choose the order of debate at the current congress. They may rewrite clumsy legislation or recommend amendments for the entire house to consider. A final purpose might be to write commendatory resolutions.

The sample time schedules that follow contrast various organizational structures.

Sample Time Schedule for a One-Day Student Congress

8:00 A.M. — 8:30 A.M.	Registration and verification of entries
8:30 A.M. —11:30 A.M.	Morning session
11:30 A.M. —12:30 P.M.	Lunch break
12:30 P.M. — 2:30 P.M.	Afternoon session
2:30 P.M. — 3:30 P.M.	Elections and Awards

Sample Time Schedule for a Two-Day Session

3:00 P.M. — 3:30 P.M.	Registration and verification of entries
3:30 P.M. — 7:30 P.M.	Session I

Second Day

8:30 A.M. —11:30 A.M.	Session II
11:30 A.M. —12:45 P.M.	Lunch break
12:45 P.M. — 3:00 P.M.	Session III
3:30 P.M. —	Joint meeting, elections, awards

At the National Student Congress, each house is in session for the length of the National NFL Tournament. This will usually be three full legislative days (in addition to committee meetings and election time) for the preliminary sessions and one additional legislative day for the final session.

Organization

The mechanics of student congress are much simpler than those of a debate tournament. However, because of its unique nature, careful attention to details will determine whether the student congress will be exciting and successful or disappointing to all.

Prior to the actual student congress, bills and resolutions should be distributed to all participating schools. NFL specifies that all schools should receive copies of the bills and resolutions that will be on the agenda at least 30 days prior to the student congress. This amount of time allows for adequate preparation by competing students and guarantees better quality of floor debate.

As students report to the congressional session, certain organizational details must be taken care of. Prior to the session, a seating chart should have been prepared that accurately represents the seating arrangement and the exact number of delegates who will be seated. Each seat should be numbered. A corresponding set of numbers should be prepared for delegates to draw as they register. The number drawn will automatically determine where the delegate will sit. Some student congresses arbitrarily assign seats ahead of time. However, in the interest of fairness, seating should be determined by a random drawing. Even if seats must be assigned ahead of time, a random drawing should be used.

A suggested "Order of Business" is printed in the *NFL Congress Manual*. Although certain legislative bodies may follow a different agenda, this one is suitable for any such group. An agenda, or order of business, is vital to insuring that all items are handled in an orderly and timely manner.

Order of Business for Student Congress

1. Invocation
2. Call to order
3. Roll call of members and confirmation of seating charts
4. Special orders
   a. Review of special rules
   b. Review of congress procedures
   c. Special announcements and questions
5. Consideration of the calendar
6. Election of Presiding Officer
7. Committee meetings (optional) may be held at a time prearranged by the District Chairperson
8. Floor debate on bills/resolutions
9. Selection of Outstanding and Most-Outstanding congress participants
10. Award of congress gavel and plaques

11. Fixing time for next meeting
12. Adjournment

Elections

Presiding Officer

The Presiding Officer conducts the assembly as efficiently and fairly as possible so that the purpose of the congress is accomplished and each member has a full chance to demonstrate his or her ability to speak and subsequently to improve. Because of this responsibility, it is important that the person chosen as the Presiding Officer be the best possible one. It is also important that the student chosen have a real desire to serve in that capacity and take pride in her or his ability to keep the group running smoothly and fairly. To insure this, students at the District Student Congress are asked to submit their names in advance for consideration as Presiding Officer. If a very large number of names is submitted, the district committee or the General Director will have to select three for each house. Each nominee for Presiding Officer will be allowed to preside for 20 to 30 minutes in rotation. Then the members of the house will select by ballot the one who will preside for the duration of the student congress. At practice congresses, the same selection process can be used.

The procedure at the National Student Congress is somewhat different. At the first session, the General Director will appoint a temporary Presiding Officer. This person will open the session, introduce the Parliamentarian and Scorer, and will then accept nominations for Presiding Officer. In most cases, there will be a nominating speech in which each candidate may present qualifications and experience that might suggest an ability to lead the group as its Presiding Officer. After all nominees have been heard, there will be an election by ballot. Each member, including the temporary Presiding Officer, writes the name of one nominee on a slip of paper. When one nominee receives a majority of the vote, the voting ceases, and the winner is announced. However, until that time, the following procedure is used. After each ballot, the person receiving the fewest number of votes (or the persons, if two or more are tied) is dropped from the list, and the members vote again. This procedure is used until one receives a majority and is declared the Presiding Officer for the session. Because the first half day at the National Student Congress is used for committee meetings, the term of office for each Presiding Officer will be one afternoon and one morning, making up a full legislative day.

There will be a total of three different Presiding Officers for each of the houses of the National Student Congress. This procedure could be used by practice congresses as well.

Although the Presiding Officer cannot be nominated for the superior representative during the session at which he or she presides, an official Congress Gavel is awarded to the student for that session. There are two reasons for excluding the Presiding Officer from consideration for superior representative. First, it should be apparent that the Presiding Officer would have higher visibility than any other member of the group. Further, the natural aura of authority that has to surround a Presiding Officer would create a kind of "halo effect" and give that person an advantage over all others who might be nominated for that session. However, more important, if the Presiding Officer is in contention for superior representative during the session in which he or she presides, his or her objectivity might be compromised. If actively competing for honors, he or she might be tempted to give recognition only to those who would not threaten his or her winning. Instead, giving the Presiding Officer an automatic award effectively removes that person from a competitive frame of mind. It is important to remember, however, that a person who has already been selected superior representative for one session may be elected Presiding Officer at another session. Conversely, a person who has served as Presiding Officer for one session may be nominated for superior member during another session.

Superior Members

Each house of the student congress selects outstanding students for awards. The nomination and election procedures that NFL outlines for practice and NFL District Congresses differ somewhat from those used at the National Student Congress. There are major differences in duration and complexity. However, the basic principle of selection is the same in all situations. The nomination for outstanding students is done by the Official Scorer and the Parliamentarian of each house, each of whom nominates a designated number of students as superior participants. The final selection of the most outstanding student from among the nominees is done by balloting all the student members of the house. The standard terminology that has developed for award winners for student congress recognizes the first place competitor as Most Outstanding, the runner-up as Outstanding, and others nominated as superior participants.

In NFL District and practice congresses, after the nominations have been made without consultation between the two officials, there is a vote at the conclusion of the congress. The same method that is used for the Presiding Officer voting is used. However, when two candidates remain, the one receiving more votes is awarded the gold plaque as Most Outstanding; the second student receives the silver plaque as Outstanding. If the student congress is the NFL District Congress, the students receiving the plaques also qualify for the National Student Congress.

At the National Student Congress, the Parliamentarian and the Scorer nominate, without consultation, two students for each legislative session. In addition, the three top point earners of the session are added if they were not nominated by either official. At the end of each legislative day, the names of all nominated students are placed on a ballot, and preferential balloting is used to determine for each Senate or House the superior representatives. These students qualify to participate in the fourth, or final, session, from which come the final award winners for the National Student Congress. In preferential balloting, each member marks all names on the ballot with numbers—for example, first through sixth place for a ballot with six candidates. Only one ballot is used to determine preferential winners. The ballots are first separated according to the first choice that is shown on each. The person receiving the lowest number of first place votes is temporarily set aside, and his or her votes are then distributed according to the second choice expressed on those ballots. The person then having the lowest number of votes is set aside, and his or her votes are redistributed. This process continues until one candidate has received a majority of the votes and is declared the winner of the balloting. The same ballots may then be used in a similar manner to determine the second most-preferred candidate once the winner's name has been removed as a further contender. The use of this method of voting insures secrecy of the results until the conclusion of the third session or, in the case of the final session, until the National Tournament Awards Session. Understanding how preferential balloting functions should make a student more aware of the importance of marking the places below first.

Summary

The rules of student congress are similar to those of the U.S. Congress, although the student congress may have more or less than two houses. The houses meet in sessions with a specific order of business. As a member, you will be responsible for knowing the bills and resolutions on the agenda prior to the session. You will also vote to elect the Presiding Officer and superior members of your house.

Chapter 4

Responsibilities of Student Congress Officials

E very student congress must have a General Director who will make arrangements and give general supervision to the entire event. Within each house of the student congress, certain officials are necessary for smooth operation. NFL rules specify that each house must have a Parliamentarian, a Chief Clerk, or both. At the National level, these are always two different persons, but at lower level student congresses, the duties may be performed by one person. An Official Scorer is also appointed for each half day of legislative session. In addition, the host school or district should provide two students to act as Pages for each house. A person responsible for timekeeping is also necessary. In addition to the appointed officials, each house of the student congress elects a Presiding Officer for each session.

General Director

The responsibilities of the General Director of a student congress are, for the most part, supervisory in nature. If the student congress is an NFL District or National Congress, then the arrangements that must be made are outlined by the rules of that organization. The General Director of a practice student congress or any student congress modeled after the NFL student congress must be aware of the many responsibilities the position carries with it.

The General Director is responsible for finding a suitable location for the congressional sessions. Experience has shown that this is a very important matter. Great effort should be exercised to find a meeting area that is not a classroom or an auditorium. If possible, the trustee board room, the city council chambers, a library, or a courtroom should be obtained. The proper location of a student congress helps produce the frame of mind in each competitor that will lead to outstanding performance. The environment should seem like a congressional meeting place.

The General Director is also responsible for securing the services of all the other student congress officials (Parliamentarian, Chief Clerk, Scorer, Pages, and Timekeeper). These persons will directly determine the success of the student congress, and the General Director should select them carefully according to the guidelines of their positions. After selecting them, the General Director should arrange to meet with them, give them written instructions, and make sure they fully understand their responsibilities and the overall activity of student congress.

The General Director is also responsible for securing awards. Each Presiding Officer must have a gavel during the session and to be presented to the Presiding Officer at the conclusion of the student congress. In addition, there should be a plaque for both the first- and second-place competitors from each house, with possible awards for all those nominated as superior participants.

Official Scorer

The Official Scorer judges student congress performances. Each legislative session has a different Scorer. The Scorer has the major responsibility for determining the relative merit of each speech and awarding points to it. In NFL and practice student congresses, there is a maximum of six points for each speech, with five or six points awarded for a superb presentation, three or four points given for an average speech, and one or two points reserved to indicate that the presentation was deficient in major areas. These point restrictions are different at the National Student Congress. Because of these restrictions, the Scorer must have a firm idea of the standards to be used in scoring, along with a clear knowledge of the rules that govern speaking in student congress. Such factors as persuasiveness, communicative delivery, innovative and effective arguments, sound reasoning and logical analysis, and incisive and knowledgeable answers to questions should weigh heavily in an Official Scorer's criteria for judging speeches. The speaker's ability to follow the flow of the debate and respond to previous speakers is also important, as is the speaker's ability to support and document assertions. In all, an Official Scorer is asked to evaluate both the content and the delivery of the speech.

The Scorer must know, in addition, that no student may speak more than five times in a legislative day unless no other delegate is asking for the floor. In addition, he or she should realize that no points can be awarded for clerical duties. The Scorer must also award points to the Presiding Officer at the end of each hour. These points should reflect the quality of the Presiding Officer's performance during that hour. The Scorer's job is difficult and demanding. It should not be accepted without careful consideration of what is involved.

At the end of the session, the Scorer will nominate an agreed-upon number of members (usually two or three) for student congress honors. These nominations, along with those submitted by the Parliamentarian, shall be voted on by the students. These nominees should be the students who have done the most outstanding job during that session. Although the Scorer awards points only for speeches that were given, every facet of the students' congress performance should be considered when making nominations.

Parliamentarian

Although the Parliamentarian's role is also supervisory, the position requires a great deal of responsibility. The person who serves in this capacity must not only know parliamentary procedure, but also be very familiar with the special rules of student congress and be willing to see that errors in procedure are immediately remedied. As a consequence, the Parliamentarian must be someone whose authority will not be questioned, but also someone who will not assert that authority until it is necessary to do so.

The Parliamentarian must have a clear understanding of the nature of student congress and must be dedicated to advancing it in the most efficient possible way. It is the Parliamentarian's primary duty to back up and reinforce the Presiding Officer. Further, the purpose of student congress is to debate legislation, and the Parliamentarian is charged with the responsibility of seeing that time is not wasted on other matters. The Parliamentarian also nominates students for honors at the conclusion of each session. He or she takes into account total contributions made to the student congress by members during that session.

An accurate record should be kept of all proceedings and, consequently, of any parliamentary problems that arise. Often, the Parliamentarian is responsible for such a record, either keeping it or delegating the responsibility to someone else. A preferred system is a dual one in which either a Clerk or a Page and the Parliamentarian both keep a written record of legislation and motions and their disposal.

Page

The Page for a house in student congress facilitates communication among the members of the house, among the Presiding Officer and members, and among the officials. The Page is, in short, a bearer of messages. He or she should be seated in an area that is easily accessible to the Presiding Officer, Scorer, and Parliamentarian. The location should also provide a clear view of the assembly so the Page can respond to a summons from a member. Excessive message sending is not to be encouraged, but notes can often allow for better working relationships and offset poor debating conditions. In addition, the Page should assist with clerical duties, such as point recording at the end of each session, passing and collecting ballots, recording motions and their disposal, and giving any other assistance to student congress officials.

Timekeeper

Because each speech is restricted to only three minutes and because accurate adherence to time limits insures fairness, a Timekeeper is an essential official in the student congress. He or she should be equipped with a stopwatch and should be instructed to use time cards. The time cards allow a speaker to see the number of minutes remaining in the speech and alert the Presiding Officer that the speaker's time is expiring. For this reason, the Timekeeper should be seated in a place that is clearly visible to the Presiding Officer, Parliamentarian, Scorer, and speaker. Strict enforcement of time limits is necessary.

Presiding Officer

The Presiding Officer for each session of student congress is elected from the membership of that group. It is absolutely essential to place a person in that position who can exert leadership. The person who is presiding must also know parliamentary procedure, must be willing to use it, and must be able to use it with authority. This does not mean that the ideal Presiding Officer is a martinet who has no interpersonal skills. It does mean that the Presiding Officer is "boss" and should be obeyed within the structure of parliamentary law. A weak Presiding Officer can wreck a student congress and waste everyone's time.

The Presiding Officer must be aware of the restrictions placed on the recognition of speakers and must apply the rules regardless of school and personal loyalties. A Presiding Officer who is not fair in giving recognition will quickly have a group of enemies in the student congress who will begin to be a negative and obstructive force. Although the Presiding Officer is in charge, it is much better to be in charge of cooperative individuals.

In addition to the recognition of speakers, the Presiding Officer is also responsible for insuring the rotation of speakers from affirmative to negative. This is usually achieved by announcing clearly each time, "The chair will now entertain a speech for the affirmative (or negative) side." Furthermore, the Presiding Officer must establish a consistent method of presiding that is clearly understood by all. For example, following each speech the chair can announce, "Procedural motions are now in order." If no one asks for recognition, the Presiding Officer can then call for the next speech. This eliminates misunderstandings of the reason a member seeks recognition. The Presiding Officer must also control time limits for speeches and must have a clear, consistent policy on stopping speakers at the conclusion of their allotted time. One of the functions of the chair's gavel comes into play at this point in the proceedings.

The Presiding Officer must make sure that a member yields only to a question and not in order to allow another member to speak. The main goal of the Presiding Officer should be to insure fairness and equity set out in the rules of student congress, such as the procedural rule specifying that no one shall be recognized to speak a second time if anyone asking for recognition has not spoken for the first time. To allow a person who receives recognition under that rule to yield speaking time to one who has already spoken would obviously circumvent the established equity. If a Presiding Officer fails to enforce such rules, he or she is subject to parliamentary moves from the assembly or to a ruling from the Parliamentarian.

In addition to a leadership role and a procedural role, the Presiding Officer must also fulfill a political role. Unfortunately in our society, the label of "politics" or "politician" has come to carry negative connotations in recent years. However, we use the term in the context of the interpersonal roles that are a necessary part of the student congress environment. The Presiding Officer must work constantly with the members of the assembly to cement and solidify relationships. He or she should be aware, for example, of the pressures under which members of the assembly are working. The Presiding Officer should be sensitive to their desire to be treated fairly but should also help them be conscious of the difficulty of the Presiding Officer's roles. Very minor, yet highly effective, strategies can make such a relationship possible. For example, the Presiding Officer may become aware of a person who has asked for recognition but has not received it and is angry. A quick note explaining that others will have to be recognized first but that the Presiding Officer is aware of the member and will get to him or her in due time may certainly alleviate the anxiety. Such an act by the Presiding Officer can take the edge off the member's frustration and keep that member from turning the frustration into a negative element in the debate ahead.

The Presiding Officer should also be aware of those in the assembly who make the job smoother and easier. The member who makes a helpful procedural motion or the one who handles a problem by suggestion rather than by challenging the Presiding Officer's authority should be acknowledged by the Presiding Officer. The member who gives a particularly outstanding speech or the one who uses valuable speaking time to clarify a rather muddled debate has also made an important contribution to the assembly. The Presiding Officer who is alert to these positive elements in the student congress should send notes or make a point of speaking to these persons during a recess. Each kind of positive move made by members of the assembly makes the performance of the Presiding Officer easier and more impressive to observers.

Interdependency is the key to a successful term as Presiding Officer of student congress. The Presiding Officer should certainly be prepared to deal with intransigent or stalemating members by using parliamentary rules properly and decisively. However, in order to fulfill an obligation to all of the assembly, school, regional, or personal loyalties should be firmly set aside when the Presiding Officer picks up the gavel.

Each official of the student congress, whether appointed or elected, has very specific and important obligations for making the student congress successful. However, these officials function within an environment governed by certain mechanics of procedure that must be clearly understood by all and that were discussed in chapters 2 and 3.

Summary

Although every student congress member plays an important part in the business, officials have special roles. The General Director, Scorer, Parliamentarian, Page, Timekeeper, and Presiding Officer all function to keep debate running smoothly and fairly. Serving in one of these offices can enhance your student congress experience.

Chapter 5

Preparation for Student Congress

Once you have a sound understanding of the principles of student congress and have mastered the mechanics of the event, you are ready to begin preparation for participation. Although most students who are part of an NFL chapter will be preparing along with the whole squad, there are a number of things you should do for yourself.

Individual Preparation

Analysis

The first step in student congress preparation is to read carefully and thoughtfully the legislation under consideration. A more global point of view is necessary for student congress analysis than for interscholastic debate analysis. The analysis of bills and resolutions for student congress must fall into the realm of what is good and best for the nation, not just what will win a debate round. A long-range view and a national perspective are important in congress debates. In your analysis, you should strive to get beyond local, partisan, or regional outlooks. This is especially important in preparation for the NFL National Student Congress, but it can be equally important in other levels of student congress.

The student congress representative from the Deep South whose only perception is a southern one may find her or his views rejected outright. He or she may suffer from a credibility gap difficult to overcome. The Texan who sees the energy crisis from the perspective of "Let the Yankees freeze to death in the dark," a sentiment expressed on some bumper stickers in that region, may alienate a large number of people quickly. And so would a student congress senator from New York who asserts that the energy situation is a fraud perpetrated by the major oil companies to hike up profits. This is not to say that these viewpoints are invalid. However, they are not the *only* valid viewpoints. You must attempt to discover many points of view prior to entry into floor debate. You may choose not to espouse them, but you must know that they exist. A purely provincial analysis will not serve you well.

Another area in which your analysis for student congress differs somewhat from that for debate is in the historical perspective. In recent years, it has become the fashion for college and high school teams to indicate in the affirmative plan that "Affirmative speeches will constitute the legislative history of this proposal." What this does, in effect, is to erase all the past history of any other attempts to adopt or reject such a proposal. Consequently, the negative's charge that the "U.S. Congress just last year voted not to fund a proposal to develop solar energy" would have no validity in the debate. Such a practice is not in vogue in student congress, however. Since the student congress attempts to function within the framework of reality, the legislative, political, and judicial history of any proposal is not only relevant, but vital to legislative consideration. If the bill to come before the student congress concerns a moratorium on spending for research and development for the Strategic Defense Initiative, a student who attempts to speak about that bill without an understanding of past arms treaties and without an understanding of the military and political relations between the United States and the Soviet Union on the issue of "Star Wars" has done a poor job of analysis of the bill.

Finally, analysis for student congress must also involve an understanding of the vested interests that are represented by the proposal. It must reflect an awareness of the ultimate effect of the adoption or rejection of the bill and of the possible compromises that may be needed to gain adoption. Having gained this understanding and awareness, you will then know what alliances will be necessary to achieve your goal. In short, the analysis of legislation for debate in student congress involves not only the proposition itself but also the interaction between advocates and opponents. It should be apparent that if there weren't these partisan positions and competing arguments, there would be no clash created and the legislation would be adopted without debate.

Research

As you analyze the bills and resolutions for student congress, you are laying the groundwork for the research process. Read everything you can find on the subjects covered. Collect as much information as you would in preparing a research paper. Talk with people whose ideas might be particularly valuable. Begin by researching generalities on the subject matter. Find out the present problem that the bill attempts to solve or that the resolution addresses. Be sure to research both sides of the question. Ultimately you might decide to give a speech either for or against the legislation. Be aware of the subject matter in the news; approach the situation as if you were an actual legislator dealing with actual legislation. Although you will not accumulate the bulk of files and evidence cards that the average debate team collects these days, you must begin with the notion that special research is necessary for thorough preparation. For this purpose, you will need to consult some sources not traditionally used by debaters. To gain a historical perspective on each bill, a good place to begin is an encyclopedia or a government textbook. Books that would probably not be quoted in a debate round hold a great deal of value for the student congress deliberation.

You must be able to speak with authority about the present as well as the past. Current magazines should be utilized (keep the *Readers' Guide to Periodical Literature* handy), with special emphasis on such publications as *Vital Speeches, Congressional Quarterly, Congressional Digest, The Congressional Record, The Congressional Quarterly Weekly Report*, and *Current History*. The value of these particular publications is their regular inclusion of actual legislative debate on issues that would be similar to those considered by the student congress. *Facts on File* for the current year, as well as for the past several years, is an important source of specific examples and statistical data. The current issue of an almanac such as *Information Please Almanac* will give up-to-date materials. If your squad maintains extemporaneous speaking files, they will have a wealth of current information on many of the bills. In addition to these sources, you may want to write to your own United States congressional representatives for materials. Personal letters, telephone conversations, newscasts, and personal interviews are admissable as evidence in student congress as long as they are accurately and carefully cited. Evidence in student congress is necessary just as it is in debate, and a great variety of sources is useful. The same care for accuracy and ethics in evidence usage must be taken in student congress as in debate.

A final note on research. After you have researched the subject matter on each bill and resolution, another area of general research will prove very valuable. Get facts and statistics together concerning the decision-making process as it relates to government spending. How much money is being spent and how much the national debt is growing are important facts and should be readily available to use in floor debate. Beyond these obvious facts, you need to know more about how the specific bills considered by the student congress fit into an overall budget picture in the current economic and fiscal situation in the nation. Be creative. Find out how much money is going into "pork barrel" projects, congressional junkets, strange research subjects, such as the mating habits of the three-toed sloth, and other areas in which government money might be said to be wasted. Investigate government bureaucracy and departmental organization. These facts might seem trivial, but they can frequently serve you well as you are pressed to demonstrate priorities. Such material injected into the floor debate can also alleviate tension through the judicious use of humor.

Organization

Once you have gathered the evidence you need for each bill and resolution, you must put it into a form that will make it easily retrievable and usable. Many students have used various methods of organizing their congress files. Two methods used with a high degree of success by students of the authors are offered here as examples.

A *vertical file* organization is flexible and easy to set up. Secure one legal-sized manila file folder for each bill or resolution. On the outside of the folder, draw a vertical line that divides the front into two equal parts. On one side, list all the arguments in favor of the bill. On the other side, list all the points against the bill. Devise a simple numerical code beside each argument, such as A–1, A–2, and so on. Place the numerical designation beside each argument. Inside the file folder, place all the evidence you have collected to support each of the points listed on the front. Each piece of evidence should be given the numerical code corresponding to the point it supports. You should laminate or glue the actual bill or resolution to the inside front cover of the file. In this way, all the pertinent materials about each bill are easily accessible for quick reference during floor debate.

A second method of organization is the use of a *loose leaf notebook*. A section is set aside for each bill or resolution by means of a divider properly labeled with the name of the item. Plastic "slick sheets" are used to hold the bill at the front of each section. Next, a section of all arguments for the bill is set up. On a sheet of paper, outline all the arguments in favor of the resolution or bill. Immediately behind that page, all evidence is entered to support those points. After the section in favor of the bill, a page of outlined arguments against the bill is placed, followed by evidence to support those points. In this kind of organization, photocopies of articles with pertinent sections underlined or highlighted can be number coded in the margin to match the section on the outlined arguments. You can also put together a series of congress briefs for each bill or resolution. Briefs contain a multitude of arguments in outline form, including interspersed evidence taken from a variety of sources. Such a brief becomes a "living document" that could be used during the floor debate. If a few of your own arguments happen to be used by one or more speakers, you could cross off those points from your brief. As new issues or challenges arise, it is easy enough to add arguments or responses onto your brief. As you seek recognition for your speech, it is easy enough to order the major points remaining on your brief and add an introduction, transitions, and a conclusion to round out the speech. The ability to speak from an outline is indispensable to this style of organization. Regardless of which method you use, remember that in congress just as in debate, citations should be shown for all evidence.

Additional kinds of organization may occur to you. Students frequently group bills by broad categories, such as Foreign Aid, Energy, or Defense. General information is then collected and filed in corresponding categories. Other students prefer to take extemporaneous speaking files into the congress meeting room. Whatever works well for you should be used. The point is that you must impose some organization on your material. The student congress competitor who arrives with a group of loose papers clutched in hand, a randomly selected magazine or two under the arm, and no clear idea of what to say is at a severe disadvantage. The student who comes with organized and well-supported positions will be able to get into the debate quickly and will give a good accounting of herself or himself in the bargain.

Preparing Speeches

After analyzing, gathering, and organizing evidence, you should carefully look at each bill and resolution to determine if you would like to offer any amendments. If so, they should be written out, and evidence should be gathered for each one and filed according to the organizational scheme you are using. Of course amendments may grow out of debate, in which case they cannot be prepared in advance. However, careful thinking about each bill may reveal several possible amendments that can be prepared and researched ahead of time.

If you have submitted a bill or resolution to the student congress, you will need to prepare your authorship speech carefully. This speech will be the first one given on the bill and will serve to introduce it to the assembly. Because the speech can be prepared ahead of time, it can and should have the careful construction and audience appeal of an oration. The authorship speech could be used to spike out the major objections that the opposition might try to voice. Anticipating and preempting arguments will make the position of the bill stronger initially and will make it more difficult for the members who wish to oppose it to find a valid argument. As with all congress speeches, the authorship speech should begin with an arresting introduction to challenge the audience, contain a well-organized body, and close with a thoughtful summary and conclusion.

Remember that during this individual preparation you will be collecting far more than you will be able to utilize in actual speaking situations in student congress. The problem is that you will not be able to anticipate just what you will get to say or the circumstances under which you will be able to say it. If you plan only one specific issue to cover only one side of a bill, you may find yourself unable to use it for a variety of reasons. The first person to get recognition may say precisely what you had planned to say, therefore effectively neutralizing your impact if you should get a chance to speak. Or it may be that a great many students wish to speak on the same side you had originally planned for, making it difficult for you to get the floor. However, no one may have been prepared to speak on the opposite side, leaving the floor wide open for you if you are suitably prepared on that side as well. Since participation is the door for success in student congress, it should be obvious that broad and careful preparation is the key to that door.

Squad Preparation

Ideally, a speech and debate squad will have several opportunities during the year to participate in practice student congresses. Sometimes, however, the only student congress of the year is the NFL District Congress. Whether student congress is a continuous event throughout the year or a once-a-year occasion, a squad working together can do a great deal to get all its members ready to participate. Squad participation in the preparation process is important even if only a few are allowed to attend because experience needs to be built for future participation.

Attitude

The most important part of a squad's preparation for student congress is the setting of attitudes. A coach should talk about and help prepare for student congress to grant it the importance that it is due. The squad should see student congress as a respected and valuable activity. A clear understanding of the principles of student congress and of the place such experience has in the forensic progression can help build those attitudes that will foster success for the individual as well as the group.

Bills and Resolutions

Each member of the squad should already have written at least one bill or resolution. There are several reasons for this. First, you will gain a great deal of understanding about analysis of a bill from doing the research necessary to produce one yourself. You will then be better able to evaluate the merits of the legislation actually used in the student congress. You will be able to detect a weak bill or one that is not in proper form. There is also the pragmatic need for practice bills for the squad practice sessions. Requiring everyone on the squad to write at least one bill will produce an ample supply for that purpose. Finally, the school will usually be required to submit at least one bill or resolution for use in the debate at student congress. The more bills the squad has to choose from, the better the quality of the bill eventually sent to the General Director of the student congress.

Once the bills have been written, it is useful for the squad to read them carefully, evaluate them as to form and substance, and make suggestions for revision. Then the squad should make some initial analysis of the bills as a group. This squad analysis gives you practice in preparation for the time when you will have to analyze the bills that will be used in the student congress in which you will compete.

Research

Squad research is another important tool. This is not to say that individuals will be excused from their own research. Quite to the contrary, each person must conduct independent analysis and research in any given area. But a certain amount of background for particular bills can be assigned to squad members who can then share the information and save time for the group. The specific arguments that you will bring up for or against a bill must then be researched by you, but the overall background of the topic will be common to all, regardless of your position on the bill.

Parliamentary Procedure

Individual students can read the parliamentary rules and review a precedence chart. But the way to achieve a working knowledge of parliamentary procedure is through practice and use. This requires a group effort, and it is one of the most important things a squad can do to prepare for student congress. After an initial review and discussion of motions, precedence, and rules, the coach should appoint a Presiding Officer, hand out a bill that has been researched, and begin a series of practice sessions in class. The coach can prescribe motions to be made at given points or can simply encourage students to experiment with all the motions. The Presiding Officer should be rotated with each new bill so that all members of the squad can learn the rudiments of presiding. In this fashion, you can find out in the relative safety of the classroom which motions can be used and what their effect on an assembly will be. A word of caution here is appropriate. Expect the first several sessions to be somewhat chaotic and confusing. This is not the fault of parliamentary procedure but rather the result of inexperience. That, in itself, should encourage a lot of practice sessions before competing in student congress. You might consider inviting a current or former member of your forensic squad with some congress experience to serve as Presiding Officer for your first practice session.

During these parliamentary practice sessions, it would be a good idea for the coach or an outside observer to score the speeches given. This will give the squad some idea of how well their speeches were structured and what each one needs to do for improvement. A clerk should also keep records of the parliamentary procedures used during these sessions so that the coach can check at the end of the session for motions that may not have been used. Through practice, the group will get a great deal of experience in the use of parliamentary rules and legislative debate. Make sure there is time and a method for debriefing after each practice session so that the experience constitutes learning, not just the repetition of mistakes. The old adage that "Practice makes perfect" might, without such a process, better be stated, "Practice makes perfectly awful!"

Rules and Regulations

In addition to practicing parliamentary procedure, the practice sessions conducted by the squad should familiarize everyone with the rules and regulations governing the congress that will be attended. Rules restricting speaking, time limits, methods of addressing the chair, and other procedural rules should be strictly enforced during practice sessions. If the squad uses these rules enough, they will learn them thoroughly. They will feel more secure in the student congress. And they will have time during student congress debates to think more about what they are going to say than about the form in which they should be speaking or other procedural considerations.

Summary

You prepare for student congress both by yourself and with your squad. On your own, you analyze and research the bills and resolutions and then organize your information. You also prepare your authorship speech or any amendments you wish to propose. As a member of a squad, you develop bills and resolutions for an upcoming congress and practice parliamentary procedure.

Chapter 6

Strategies for Success in Student Congress

I f you plan and prepare to participate in a student congress, you will, of course, aspire to succeed in the activity. But, although your advance understanding and thorough preparation are major determinants of success, these elements are only the first steps. Your actual conduct and your attitude during the student congress are the variables that make student congress participation such a challenge. We have interviewed many successful participants about their impressions of the attitudes and actions most likely to contribute to effectiveness in student congress. Based on their experiences, we offer some suggestions that may be useful to future student congress members. This collection of suggestions is not meant to constitute a money-back guarantee for election to Outstanding Congress Member. Your own personality as well as the past relationships that you have had in competition with others in the student congress will affect how well a particular strategy will work for you.

Attitude

Legislative debate is a challenging and rewarding experience for a forensic student. The person who approaches student congress as if it were a step down from debate insults not only the activity but the other participants as well. Such an attitude is usually apparent and will result in immediate and far-reaching negative attitudes from others. If you want to be a successful congress member, you must treat student congress as an event important and respected in its own right. You should demonstrate by actions and words that you care about the activity, that you are prepared to work, and that you see value in the event, regardless of outcome.

The most successful student congress member also approaches student congress as an enjoyable event and works to make it that kind of experience. Such attitudes are evidenced in many ways during the sessions of congress. Promptness in reporting to committee sessions and paying close attention to the task of the committee can indicate the importance that you attach to the activity. Listening carefully to other members during house debate shows enthusiasm and support for those who have the floor and allows you to participate in cross-examination to contribute to the progression of the debate. A positive and concerned attitude should be evidenced at all times by all participants.

Interpersonal Skills

Closely related to the attitude you have as a participant is your ability to relate to and work with others. In no other area of forensic competition is the success of the event directly dependent on how well the competitors work together. Consequently, your ability to work with others and to construct good relationships with them is very important. No one would be naive enough to suggest that the members of a student congress gather together just for the purpose of being nice to one another. It is understood that this is a competitive activity. However, you need to understand that the competition is achieved through the ability of speakers to debate bills and resolutions, not through attacks on the personalities of the participants.

Because developing positive interpersonal relationships is important to the success of the student congress, you should begin early to work on these. If you are the only representative from your school, then you will doubly need to form acquaintances with others, beginning as early as registration. Often, particularly at an NFL District Student Congress, you will be among others with whom you have competed during the year in other events. There may be an understandable residue of hostility or at least reserve among the group. Efforts should be made to set aside those attitudes and to begin fresh with the student congress. One thing to avoid in the early period of the student congress is the tendency to stay among participants from your own school or region. It is important for you to circulate, to learn names, and to begin to build relationships.

One student who was named Most Outstanding Congressperson at the NFL National Student Congress indicated that he believed that high visibility as soon as possible is important, especially at the national level, where very few students know one another. This visibility is necessary to the building of interpersonal relationships. It can be achieved in a variety of ways. Being direct and gregarious early in the session, learning the names of others by introducing yourself, asking questions, and giving others an opportunity to respond will all give you visibility. Casual conversation during recesses and at meal time can also promote visibility. One student congressmember observed that these times of talking about everything else except student congress probably had more to do with achieving effectiveness than any debate on the floor. And she was probably correct in terms of building good relationships and giving students an opportunity to appraise each other's ability.

Committee work is another time to build visibility early in the session. Volunteer to chair the committee and then be efficient and pleasant in the work of that committee. You will build a nucleus of student congress colleagues who know and respect you. In addition, you will have made a positive contribution to the success of the student congress itself.

Politics

The United State Congress is a political institution, and members of student congress are no less susceptible to playing politics than their counterparts in Washington, D.C. However, you should exercise much caution, for as national events have dramatically illustrated in recent years, the game of politics can be hazardous.

As a member of student congress, you should realize from the outset that in spite of your best efforts there will be a degree of partisanship or polarization even before debate begins. Some of this has already been alluded to. You may be able to mitigate it, but you will probably never be able to erase all preexisting animosities stemming from rivalries developed during the competitive season. Several personality conflicts or personal rivalries will probably exist, certainly at the district and practice level. In addition, there may be regional prejudice even at the national level, or a residue of animosity built on differences at earlier student congresses. Finally there will be some members who arrive determined to get their pet bill passed, regardless of the consequences or the methods used to accomplish this end.

Almost every successful former student congress delegate whom the authors interviewed had one absolute word of advice about the politics that such conditions as these create. Their advice was simple: "Stay out of it if possible!" It was the feeling of these former competitors that they served their own best interests and those of the student congress simply by listening with an open mind to the efforts of others to pull them into one group or another and then by simply moving on without making a commitment. There may be some plots laid, even some that are somewhat underhanded, in an effort to destroy a bill or to undermine the credibility of some student who supports a particular piece of legislation. Avoiding such plots and working only for the betterment of debate on the floor is a much better strategy for success.

Perhaps the best way to approach the possibility of politics in the student congress setting would be the one most of us would hope to see followed in the legislatures of our own state or nation. Align yourself with people and causes only after careful study has determined that the cause is worthy and the people are sincere. Overall, the successful student congress members we interviewed felt that political power plays and behind-the-scenes plots did little in the long run to advance the cause of the persons involved. Several interviewees cited examples of promising student congress members who were seriously damaged by involvement in such schemes.

An additional caution: If you get frustrated at the political wheelings and dealings of your session, you become your own worst enemy. If you constantly seem to be saying "It's just not fair" or "The system is against me," then the danger is that you will either pull back or react in anger. Instead, decide on a method of coping that will not be destructive either to yourself or to the group.

Debate

The strategies for success in floor debate are almost all predicated on adequate preparation and persuasiveness in presentation. It is in the actual act of standing to speak as a participant in the floor debate that you are able to get NFL points, to gain greater visibility among your peers, and to put yourself in a position in which you can command their respect. As a consequence, the strategies for successful debating are vital to the success you may achieve.

Perhaps the most important thing to remember is the limitations on participation. For each session, if you are fortunate, you will get to speak a maximum of five times—and for only three minutes per occasion. Frequently, you will have fewer opportunities. As a result, it is important to be aware of the speaking that is done in the context of the total event. It is also important to realize that although every speech given does not have to be a haymaker, the higher the quality of the speech given, the better the possibility that you will find support for yourself and your position in the assembly. Is evidence given to support assertions and generalizations? Is the argument relevant to the point being made? Is the material structured so that it can be easily understood? Be sure to review the standards for judging the quality of speeches that were specified for the Official Scorer in Chapter 4 to help you gain an insight into successful styles for legislative debate speeches. For example, while a one-minute speech in itself is not unsatisfactory, how do you think it will be judged by the Scorer in comparison to other speeches?

Sometimes it is wise to try to deliver one of the first speeches for or against a bill or resolution; sometimes it is good to listen to the debate for a while before seeking recognition to speak. Listening first allows you to evaluate sides of the issue, to determine which may be the prevailing side, and to set up your own strategy of clashing with the opposition in the debate. Not all the former competitors agreed about which strategy is best. In fact, most of them discovered they had used a little of each. Certainly, success breeds success. The highly competitive student congress participant might want to wait until he or she can be sure of the side that will win and then give a speech favoring that side, extending the arguments and adding clincher arguments or evidence.

On the other hand, it might be best to accept the challenge of attempting to lead the group in the formulation of opinion. This can be achieved by getting early recognition and attempting to build the bandwagon effect in the assembly. Or, after observing the tide of opinion to one side, the challenge might be to attempt to construct a speech for the side that is losing and to make it a speech so persuasive that it would turn the direction of opinion. Either of these strategies is based on the principle inherent in all debate that either side has valid issues that can be supported by evidence.

Another way to add to the strength of a speech given during debate is to utilize speeches already given by referring to them and making your speech an extension and amplification of them. If, for example, the speaker has simply made a reference to an idea that you see as a potentially strong argument, and if you have the data by which to make it into a fully developed point, you can simply say, "Representative Green's point about the historical significance of this bill is well taken, and I would like to . . . ." Referring to other speeches can actually make your own speech sound more substantive than you could otherwise make it in only three minutes. The practical effect is that you use their data, already introduced, as a springboard to your own position. You gain time and impact. Overall, most Scorers look for clear evidence of a spontaneous clash as opposed to a series of unrelated, memorized, pre-prepared orations.

Playing out the newly discovered role of a congressional representative and employing the inherent speaking style is a part of the strategy for use in floor debate. Perhaps the most difficult thing for the debater-turned-student-congressperson to do is to regain the skills of persuasive public address after a season of debating with her or his nose in a flow pad, speaking at a rate of 400 words-per-minute. However, if you want success in student congress, then style must be a part of your delivery. The stylistic considerations that you should make involve not only the traditional use of vocal variety, gestures, vocal intonation, and appropriate volume and pauses, but also sensitivity to the times when a little humor would be a welcome relief, especially if the humor can be used to make a valid point. Examples, analogies, similes, metaphors, paradoxes, and other rhetorical devices, when used properly, are always effective in a congress speech. You should be able to sense when there is an opening for emotional as well as intellectual appeal. Further, you should be alert to moments in the debate when a carefully proposed compromise might swing two factions into agreement and bring about the passage of a particularly hard-fought piece of legislation. These are decisions that must be made at the moment and cannot be prescribed by any other person.

Summary

There are several keys to a successful student congress session. When you prepare for the session and then participate with a positive attitude, you are doing your part to make the session go smoothly. Developing your interpersonal skills is another way you can ensure a successful session. Finally, knowing the rules governing debate and following the arguments carefully can enhance everyone's student congress experience.

In these chapters you have examined the widespread and valuable activity of student congress. You should now have a better notion of its nature and purpose and of the principles that govern it. The structure of the congress activity gives specific responsibilities to the officials and also carries obligations to the participants. You have been given here, too, a clear description of the mechanics of the student congress as well as a careful guide to your own preparation for competition.

The student congressmember who approaches the experience with adequate preparation, with a thorough understanding of the event, and with a dedication to the value of the experience will probably find the strategies for success discussed here a natural outgrowth of her or his own attitudes toward student congress. In the authors' experiences, this event is a true blending of the best of all the forensics events. Perhaps the essence of student congress was best expressed in the March 1978 issue of the National Forensic League *Rostrum* by the late Bruno E. Jacob, Executive Secretary Emeritus of NFL. He said:

> In the student congress the students learn to think about state and national problems in terms of solutions which they can urge their colleagues to accept as necessary and practical. They learn how to influence people favorably. They acquire not only knowledge of lawmaking, but respect for the power of the majority and the rights of the minority—the foundations of the democratic process. This makes leaders.

Part Two

Lincoln-Douglas Debate

Confronting Value Decisions

Lincoln-Douglas debate has been a national event since 1980. It was created by the National Forensic League to offer forensic students an alternative to the fast-paced style of team debate. Lincoln-Douglas debate has its roots in the famous debates staged between Stephen Douglas and Abraham Lincoln during the 1852 Illinois State Senate race. Since then, the Lincoln-Douglas format has been limited largely to political debates. The Lincoln-Douglas format allows two speakers ample time to express their views. It has long served our need for the exchange of ideas on important issues of the day.

This section will introduce you to the principles and organization of Lincoln-Douglas debate. You will learn about value propositions. You will also learn a number of affirmative and negative techniques for successful Lincoln-Douglas debating.

Chapter 7

The Structure of Lincoln-Douglas Debate

C ertain assumptions underlie all forms of debate—the presentation of arguments, confrontation, and the use of evidence. However, particular forms of debate are affected by time constraints and the nature of the proposition.

Speaker Times

Because the Lincoln-Douglas form of debate involves only two people, the times allotted are much shorter than for team debate. The following table shows the times allotted to speakers in a Lincoln-Douglas debate.

Affirmative Constructive	6 minutes
Cross-Examination (Negative vs. Affirmative)	3 minutes
Negative Constructive	7 minutes
Cross-Examination (Affirmative vs. Negative)	3 minutes
First Affirmative Rebuttal	4 minutes
Negative Rebuttal	6 minutes
Second Affirmative Rebuttal	3 minutes

Preparation times for speakers vary according to the particular tournament. Usually, prep time is five minutes per person for the entire debate.

Although the time blocks in a Lincoln-Douglas round are not the same for the affirmative and negative speakers, the total time allotted to each side for speaking and cross-examination is the same. The affirmative has less time to establish its constructive case than does the negative. This allows the negative to respond to specific arguments introduced by the affirmative and to offer additional materials and issues in the first speech. The affirmative has a shorter amount of time for each rebuttal speech, but the affirmative's total amount of rebuttal time is longer than the negative's.

These format differences mean that speaker strategies for team debate are not necessarily effective in Lincoln-Douglas debate. There is no negative block. The first affirmative rebuttal can be a thorough, well-organized response to negative arguments, rather than a scramble to cover all aspects of the negative attack. Also, because there is no partner to pick up arguments, Lincoln-Douglas debaters have to assume a greater accountability for their debating.

Tournament Procedures

Every Lincoln-Douglas tournament may be run a little differently. Some may last two or three days, while others may last only an afternoon. However, all tournaments will have certain common elements.

You will always know the debate topic in advance. In a Lincoln-Douglas tournament, you also will be expected to debate both the affirmative and negative sides of the topic. You will be assigned an identification code. It may be a number, letter, or just your last name. The code prevents a judge from identifying your school and possibly being prejudiced against you. The code is also used for postings. Postings list the debates, rooms, and times. Because Lincoln-Douglas debates run only about 40 minutes, two may be scheduled in the same room during the time period allotted to one team debate round. A sample posting is listed below.

Affirmative	Negative	Room	Time
10	15		
		B–19	9:30
20	22		

In the sample posting, two affirmatives, numbers 10 and 20, and two negatives, numbers 15 and 22, are scheduled in the same room at 9:30. This means that the first line of codes—numbers 10 and 15—debates first at 9:30, and then numbers 20 and 22 debate immediately after. You want to make sure that you are on time for your debate. Even if you are scheduled to debate the second section, you may be asked to debate ahead of time if someone from the first section drops out.

Summary

The format of Lincoln-Douglas debate differs from that of standard team debate. Since only one speaker debates on a side, there is a greater emphasis on individual accountability during the debate. Also, the shorter time limits imposed on the speakers mean that Lincoln-Douglas debaters must develop new strategies to cover the issues effectively. The other major difference between Lincoln-Douglas and standard debate is the nature of the proposition being debated. Value propositions are discussed in the next chapter.

Chapter 8

Debating Value Propositions

There are three types of debate proposition: fact, policy, and value. Propositions of fact are easily recognized and debated. They are judged to be either true or false. For example, "Capital punishment is an effective deterrent to homicide" is a proposition of fact. An affirmative debater would give evidence to support a correlation between the use of capital punishment and a reduction in homicide rates. If the affirmative can show such a link, then he or she will have proven the proposition true.

Propositions of policy concern something that is desirable or undesirable. For example, "Capital punishment should be used against all murderers" is a proposition of policy. An affirmative debater would give reasons why capital punishment should be instituted. He or she would argue that capital punishment is a desirable form of punishment and thus is an appropriate policy to adopt.

What Is a Value Proposition?

Propositions of value are inherently different from propositions of fact or policy. Value propositions involve attitudes and beliefs, not simply facts or policies. The *Oxford English Dictionary* defines *value* as "something of worth, to be highly regarded or held in great esteem." In terms of debate, a value is a belief. You may believe in the value of helping a neighbor or donating money to charity. At the same time, you may believe that being lazy or selfish is undesirable. These values can be discussed, debated, and argued, but they can never be proven true or false. This is the most important aspect of value discussion. You may, for example, believe in the value of a strong military. You can explain your belief by discussing its importance, effectiveness, necessity, or even social acceptability, but you can never prove its truthfulness.

Values are debated in terms of a specific situation. Consider the topic

"Resolved: Gun control is unjustifiable." The debaters will clash over the value of gun control. The affirmative may offer arguments designed to show that owning guns is a good, or positive, value. The arguments might include the following points:

1. "Gun control is unconstitutional."

Such a statement is designed to show that because gun control is unconstitutional, or illegal, it should therefore be considered unjustifiable.

2. "Guns are sometimes necessary for personal protection."

This statement is designed to demonstrate that people have a right to protect themselves, in this case by owning a gun. It correlates with the constitutional argument and therefore appeals to the same illegal/ unjustifiable argument but with more pathos or emotion.

3. "Many people use guns for sport and recreation."

This statement is designed to eliminate any possible negative attitudes the judge may have toward guns by showing that they can be fun and safe. It would seem unjustifiable to want to limit or control something that can provide enjoyment in a safe manner.

The negative speaker will argue against the topic by showing the value of gun control to be justified. He or she may make the following arguments:

1. "We currently allow for some gun control to insure that felons cannot purchase guns."

This statement contradicts the affirmative's first point by stating that, properly used, gun control does not violate the intent of the constitution and therefore should not be considered unjustifiable.

2. "Many senseless deaths occur from the improper use of guns."

This statement seems to hold two values in contrast: the value of the constitutional right to bear arms as opposed to the value of human life. In developing this argument, the negative would need to state clearly that these two values do not have to be in opposition, and that people can maintain their constitutional rights while knowing how to handle guns safely.

Specific propositions of value are debated in relation to general, more universal values. The real conflict in a debate of values is the hierarchy of those values—how they are ranked—and how they are linked to other values. In the preceding example of gun control, the affirmative linked the idea of eliminating gun control to the values stated in the U.S. Constitution and to the value of enjoyment.

In order for any of these arguments to be persuasive, you would need to provide information and further analysis. But you can see that values are debated in practical terms. They may be debated in terms of such ideas as illegality, enjoyment, and morality, but never in terms of being true or false. Also, as you have seen, values are debated in reference to a topic. Each topic carries its own set of relevant values that can be debated.

Types of Value Propositions

There are four types of propositions that are frequently debated in Lincoln-Douglas debate. The first two are value propositions: value conflict and value judgment. The other two types are related to value propositions; they are quasi-policy and quasi-factual propositions. All four types of propositions require slightly different approaches.

Value Conflict Propositions

Value conflict propositions are centered around a hierarchy in which values are in conflict. For example, in the topic "Resolved: Competition is of greater value than cooperation," the value of competition is in direct conflict with the value of cooperation. The affirmative may suggest that the definition of the word *value* is "degree of success." The affirmative would then show that competition is of greater value than cooperation in terms of "degree of success." The affirmative could use different analogies, ranging from the individual student striving to do his or her best, to major industries competing with one another and thereby creating better products. The overall idea behind the value conflict proposition is that two values are compared to see which is better in terms of the affirmative interpretation of the topic.

Analyzing Value Conflict Propositions

The following examples illustrate how you could analyze a value conflict proposition and plan both an affirmative and a negative strategy.

1. Resolved: Honesty is of greater value than loyalty.

In the first topic, a conflicting situation can be found in the Iran-Contra hearings. Lt. Colonel Oliver North would be a prime negative example. He stated categorically that he had lied to Congress in order to remain loyal to and protect his superiors. Using North as an example, you could examine the values of honesty and loyalty and assess, in terms of national security, which is of greater value. The definition of the value term *greater value* is crucial.

One affirmative approach would be to present a situation in which the two values are so clearly in conflict that one must take precedence in order for the situation to be resolved. As an affirmative, you would use an example to demonstrate that when the value you are defending takes precedence, the conflict is resolved with great success.

A popular negative approach for value conflict resolutions is to show that the two values are equal, and that therefore the resolution itself is false. As a negative speaker, you can use this approach to keep yourself out of difficult situations. You have to take a side. However, it is much easier to defend two time-honored values than it is to defend one while attacking the other.

2. Resolved: Guided justice is superior to blind justice.

The second proposition uses a variation of value conflict by comparing the same value word, *justice,* with two modifiers, *guided* and *blind.* In essence, these are two forms of the same value, "justice." By offering a pragmatic definition of the value term *superior,* you will be able to set up a scenario in which to view these two forms of justice. Defining *superior* as "better than" does not enable anyone to compare the two types of justice accurately. Defining *superior* as "better able to uphold the value of a fair and speedy trial" helps to establish a pragmatic scenario that is easily understood.

Value Judgment Propositions

The second type of value proposition is the value judgment proposition. This type of proposition examines whether a particular value judgment is an accurate way of describing a specific aspect of the topic. Under the topic "Resolved: Rock and roll music is horrible," rock and roll music is evaluated in terms of the definition of the word *horrible.* The affirmative would give reasons why rock and roll is horrible, and the negative would show why it is not. In this type of topic, there is no comparison of values. Instead one value is applied to a specific aspect of the topic.

Analyzing Value Judgment Propositions

The following example illustrates how you could analyze a value judgment proposition. In the resolution "Resolved: There is no such thing as a just war," the value being debated is "war." A highly specific definition or understanding of war is essential. Most people would accept that World Wars I and II were wars. And most people would agree that the conflict in Vietnam was a war, even though it was never officially declared a war by the United States government. Is war then simply the organized killing of people between two or more countries? Then what about civil wars? There are also "cold wars," in which no one is killed but countries are not on speaking terms. When Japan attacked Pearl Harbor, the United States was not officially at war with Japan. Could the attack be considered warfare? Clearly, it is extremely important—and sometimes very difficult—to define value terms in value judgment propositions.

Quasi-Policy and Quasi-Factual Propositions

The last two types of propositions applicable to Lincoln-Douglas debate are quasi-policy and quasi-factual propositions. A quasi-policy proposition does not advocate a specific plan of action or policy, but it implies one. For example, in the proposition "Resolved: Increased restriction of immigration into the United States is morally justifiable," the implied policy is that there should be more restriction of immigration. Because there is an implied policy, the negative may debate certain types of implied policy arguments. The negative may suggest that the affirmative is against letting in more immigrants and may suggest some possible harms, such as the United States being unable to live up to its moral obligation to take in people who wish to come here.

The second type of non-policy proposition is the quasi-factual proposition. A purely factual proposition is difficult to debate because it is fairly easy to prove if the proposition is true or false. However, some quasi-factual propositions are worded in such a way that they are debatable, such as "Resolved: Protectionism is a positive trade policy for U.S. industry."

Analyzing Quasi-Policy and Quasi-Factual Propositions

The following examples illustrate how you could analyze quasi-policy and quasi-factual propositions for Lincoln-Douglas debate.

1. Resolved: Governmental invasion of individual privacy is justifiable.

In this topic, *justifiable* is clearly the value term. In any policy evaluation resolution, you must be careful not to get muddled in pure policy argumentation. It can become easy to debate the policies themselves and not the values implied within the policies—that is, when and where the invasion of privacy occurs, and what type of invasion it is. These are essential elements to know, but they can best be discussed in the definitions. This debate should focus on whether the government has any reasonable purpose in usurping the constitutional right to privacy. An example could be mandatory drug testing for transportation personnel. Drug testing may be considered by some to be an invasion of privacy, but such testing could also be in the best interests of the public. The debate would be about the value of the individual's constitutional right to privacy versus the value of the greater good for the majority. Not all quasi-policy topics are as clear as this one is.

2. Resolved: Protectionism is a positive trade policy for U.S. industry.

The value term in this topic is *positive.* A basic definition of *positive* is "effective or helpful." Obviously, as applied to U.S. industry, this definition refers to economics—more people working. However, such a debate may degenerate from the implied value of protectionism, that is, protecting U.S. employment, to whether or not protectionism will actually accomplish anything. A policy's workability should not be an issue in value debate. What should be debated by the affirmative is that protectionism will insure American jobs. The negative should argue that protectionism stifles competition and therefore creates complacency. Unless you are a careful debater, such a topic could easily become a policy debate.

3. Resolved: American foreign policy in the Middle East has lost direction and purpose.

This topic is the most difficult to debate because of two problems. First, the value term is not stated but implied: losing direction and purpose is generally considered to have negative implications. As a debater, you can reasonably assume that the framers of this resolution meant that a lack of direction is bad. You may have to make such assumptions when a topic is not worded more explicitly.

Second, this topic is more a proposition of fact than of value. In other words, it merely states that something is true. Consequently, many affirmatives would assert that they should win the round once they have shown an example of American foreign policy that seems to lack direction and purpose. However, the affirmative is not excused from discussing values just because the topic is somewhat misleading in its wording. As the affirmative speaker, you have an unstated burden of proof to show that a policy with no direction is in fact bad, evil, or disastrous. If you debate only facts or examples and do not debate values, then you are living up to only half of your responsibilities.

Wording Value Propositions

There has been much discussion in both high school and college debate about how to word a proposition of value. The first difficult issue is that of presumption, the idea that if everything is equal during a debate, then the negative should win because the affirmative has not given a compelling enough argument for adopting his or her interpretation of the topic. In other words, it is assumed that the affirmative advocates some kind of change and the negative defends the present system. Unless the affirmative provides a significant reason to change from the present system, then the judge should vote for the negative, or to uphold the present system. In the topic "Resolved: The two-party system is detrimental to democratic ideals," the affirmative clearly opposes the present system. Therefore, the affirmative has the burden of proof. Burden of proof means that the speaker must present reasonable arguments to support his or her claims about the topic. The affirmative must firmly establish reasons for the judge to believe the resolution.

The difficulty lies in topics that are worded to imply no change—such as "Resolved: The two-party system is advantageous to democratic ideals"—or in topics that obscure which side is supporting the present system—such as "Resolved: Capital punishment is justified." The problem of presumption becomes even more difficult when the topic is something like "Resolved: Honesty is a greater value than loyalty." In such a topic there is clearly no present system of beliefs. You would have a difficult time proving that a majority of Americans believe in either the value of honesty above loyalty or that of loyalty above honesty. What should be done, then, to insure that presumption is with the negative?

The most important rule to keep in mind is that the initiator of an argument has the burden of proof, and that therefore the defender has the presumption. This usually means that the affirmative has the burden of proof and the negative the presumption. However, the negative can assert his or her case against the topic. In such a situation, the negative speaker would have to prove that his or her interpretation of the topic is acceptable.

Another common problem in wording Lincoln-Douglas propositions is determining if the topic is actually a "value" topic. As mentioned earlier, there are four styles of proposition that are appropriate for Lincoln-Douglas topics. Once an appropriate style has been determined, it is important to make sure that the topic is actually debatable.

Debatability hinges on whether both sides have an equal chance of winning. A topic like "Resolved: Censorship is a horrible affront to all that is pure and American" would be difficult for any affirmative to win because of the severity of the language. Another check for debatability is whether there is sufficient evidence available for the topic. This is especially important for leagues that debate three topics a year. There is little time to do comprehensive research. It is essential that the topic be easily researched in a short amount of time, and that evidence be readily available on both sides of the resolution.

Summary

One of the key differences between Lincoln-Douglas and standard debate is the debate of propositions of value, rather than propositions of policy. Value propositions involve beliefs, which cannot be proven true or false or even ranked absolutely. There are two types of value propositions: value conflict and value judgment. Value propositions must be worded carefully to insure that presumption, burden of proof, and debatability are inherent in them.

Chapter 9

The Affirmative Position in Lincoln-Douglas Debate

I n standard debate, certain stock, or essential, issues are usually covered by the affirmative team. If these issues are not covered, the negative may argue that the affirmative has not fulfilled its requirements for the debate and should lose.

Until very recently, there were no agreed upon stock issues in Lincoln-Douglas debate. However, debate theorists are beginning to believe stock issues are as important to Lincoln-Douglas as they are to team debate. There are three generally accepted stock issues for the affirmative speaker. First, the affirmative must define the object of evaluation, or *value term*, in the debate. Second, the affirmative must establish the *value criterion*—whatever the affirmative believes to be the most important value related to the topic. The value criterion is often supported by the definitions of key terms in the topic, as well as by the topic analysis. The value criterion is usually implied rather than stated directly in the resolution. For example, the topic "Resolved: Capital punishment is justified" might imply a value criterion of "revenge" on the one hand or "how to best reduce future violent crimes" on the other.

The last affirmative stock issue is *value justification*, the use of arguments to support the value criterion. The affirmative speaker must consider the consequences of applying the value criterion to the object of evaluation. The burden of proof in the debate is considered to rest with the affirmative, just as it does in team debate. If the affirmative speaker fails to address all three of these stock issues, the negative could argue that the affirmative has not upheld its burden of proof, and the judge could rule for the negative.

Affirmative Constructive

Defining the Value Term

All definitions and new arguments in Lincoln-Douglas debate must be presented in the constructive speeches. The affirmative is generally responsible for setting the definitions for the debate, although the negative may challenge those definitions. Definitions provide a framework for analysis by placing limits on the interpretation of the topic.

In debating the topic "Resolved: Governmental invasion of individual privacy is justifiable," the terms *governmental, invasion, individual privacy,* and *justifiable* would need to be defined. The first three terms are limitations that enable the debaters to focus on the most important aspects of the topic. The affirmative could not possibly discuss all aspects of the topic in just six minutes. If the terms are not defined to limit the focus of the debate, then neither the judge, your opponent, nor probably even you will know exactly what is being evaluated or examined.

The next term in the sample topic is *justifiable.* This term is the *value term.* The value term is a major part of the value criterion. Its function is to enable your opponent and the judge to evaluate what you believe the topic is all about. Therefore, the definition of the value term should be as precise as possible. In the individual privacy topic, defining *justifiable* as "acceptable" does not help your opponent or the judge understand what you believe to be the best measurement of the topic.

The value term may be a person, thing, concept, or anything else that can be defined. The importance of carefully defining the value term is clear in the topic "Resolved: Modern art is wonderful." In this topic, the value term is the two-word phrase "modern art." The ambiguity of this phrase shows how crucial the value term is to the debate as a whole. Does "modern art" refer only to art created within the last year or within the last fifty years? Does it refer only to a specific style of art, perhaps abstract painting? Does "modern art" refer only to art created by a few artists? Defining the value term is essential to a clear understanding of what is being debated.

The precise definition of the value term can be considered a stock issue because it is essential to a prima facie, or complete, case. Without it, the judge may not be able to evaluate the debate objectively. Debating the value of something, such as whether rock and roll music is better than jazz, is very difficult. You have your own feelings and so does the judge. The judge tries not to allow his or her own feelings about rock and roll to interfere with the decision. However, if you don't tell the judge how you think rock and roll should be compared to jazz (by defining the value term *better*), then you are not fulfilling your duty as the affirmative speaker. You are also gambling that the judge will feel the same as you do about rock and roll, and that may not be the case.

As you can see, it is very important to define the value term accurately. One final example illustrates this point. Many debaters only define the value term with general definitions. A real-life example illustrates the danger of not being specific. In a regional competition, the topic was "Resolved: Capital punishment is justified." The affirmative would define the value term *justified* as meaning "acceptable to society." However, the argument in the case was that capital punishment reduced crime. The affirmative debater was therefore attempting to support two values: the defined value of societal acceptance and the unstated value of reducing crime. Chances are that the affirmative speaker was not even aware of advocating two values.

While you can have more than one value to justify a topic, you need at least one fully developed argument for each value. In the capital punishment case, though, the affirmative's arguments, or value justification, usually did not support the value term, and therefore the case was not a prima facie, or complete, case. If the affirmative had defined *justified* as "related to reducing crime," then the case would have been prima facie. It would have met the two stock issues of clearly defining the value term and offering appropriate value justification in the form of arguments.

When writing a case, consider that you are building a house. The first thing to construct is your foundation. The foundation is the definitions of the limiting terms. Your foundation supports the walls, or arguments. Your arguments support the roof, or topic. Obviously, a weak definition will give little support to the topic, while a strong definition will outlast any negative assaults. The value term is then applied to see if your interpretation is strong. Naturally, you will not ask the judge to view your interpretation in light of its weakest points; that is for the negative to mention. You will want to present your case in the most positive terms possible. A solid value term will greatly enhance the judge's impression of your case.

Value Justification

The next aspect of the affirmative constructive is the arguments. Without arguments you cannot defend your interpretation of the topic, especially your interpretation of the value term. For this reason, arguments are considered the second affirmative stock issue: *value justification*.

Value justification can take many forms. You might offer authoritative proof. This can be factual evidence from magazines, newspapers, books, interviews, television, or any other source of authoritative information. Another method of justification is the use of analogies or comparisons. There is a more detailed description of evidence and analysis in the chapter on evidence.

Much like team debate, Lincoln-Douglas arguments are constructed through evidence and analysis. However, in Lincoln-Douglas debate the emphasis is often much different. You will not be expected to have as highly detailed and substructured a case as you would in team debate, but you will be expected to present a well-organized case. For example, using the topic "Resolved: Gun control is unconstitutional," you might structure your argument like this:

1. Read the Second Amendment, which allows citizens the right to bear arms.

2. Read a short quote stating that gun control is a violation of a citizen's rights.

3. Stipulate that because one has the right to bear arms, gun control is unjustified.

This is only a brief outline of three major ideas. In order to develop this outline into a six-minute case, you would need definitions, evidence, and much more analysis.

Cross-Examination

Lincoln-Douglas debate includes two cross-examination periods. The first cross-examination is conducted by the negative; the second is conducted by the affirmative. As in standard cross-examination debate, the first general rule of the cross-examination period is that the person who is questioning should be sure only to ask questions. The examiner should never make statements. Even though you may be tempted to make statements, you should save them until your next speech.

The second general rule of cross-examination is that its purpose is to clarify information and probe for weaknesses. You may not have heard everything that was said, so you will want to be sure to ask about whatever points you missed. After filling in the missing information, you will want to begin exposing weaknesses in your opponent's thoughts. Weaknesses can range from poor use of evidence to illogical analysis. Though there are many similarities between team and Lincoln-Douglas cross-examination, there is one area that is unique to Lincoln-Douglas: the questioning of values. Especially if the negative speaker has chosen to present a negative case, you will want to expose any conflicts between the negative's arguments and the value criterion of the debate.

Affirmative Rebuttals

Unlike in standard and cross-examination debate, the affirmative is the first rebuttalist in Lincoln-Douglas debate. The affirmative also has two rebuttals to the negative's one.

First Affirmative Rebuttal

For the first rebuttal, the objective is to cover as many negative arguments as possible, as well as covering your own. Pay careful attention to your value term, making sure to defend against any negative attacks, since this is the judging criterion you wish to be used. In the affirmative rebuttals, you should concentrate on repairing any damage to your case inflicted by the negative speaker.

Repairs may be simply answering a question, reading more evidence, restating, or reaffirming. If the negative only questioned your evidence, a simple response may be enough to satisfy the inquiry. It is a good idea to have new evidence ready for rebuttals, in case the negative has attacked your evidence as biased or incomplete. You do not want to disregard your original evidence, but by offering further quantification you help to remove any doubt about the integrity of your arguments. If your contentions have not been attacked, then you will need to restate and reaffirm them. For example, you may simply restate, "The negative said nothing about contention No. 2—that gun control is harmful to sportsmen." This *restatement* helps the judge to know exactly which point you are discussing and reaffirming. The *reaffirmation* helps the judge to better understand the merit of a particular argument.

Second Affirmative Rebuttal

You have only three minutes in the final rebuttal. You probably cannot cover adequately all the arguments in this amount of time, assuming the negative has responded to everything you have said. This is when the four-step pattern of restatement will help you. The four steps are:

1. State where you are in the debate.

2. Restate your opponent's response.

3. State your response.

4. Summarize the impact of the argument on the debate.

The steps allow you to focus on the case issues you are winning and also to point out the issues on which you believe you have beaten the negative. Such attention to organization is very important. It is a means of making sure you have responded adequately to all attacks and have extended your case reasonably throughout the debate. It is also important because it improves your personal speaking style. In your last speech, you do not want to leave the judge with the impression that you are poorly organized. Style can be a key factor in some debates. Imagine yourself as a judge. Who would you vote for: Someone who was so disorganized she or he had to ask you what arguments to discuss, or someone who was so confident and organized that he or she actually seemed to guide you through the debate?

Summary

Reading a textbook about how to debate may not answer all the questions you have. Such a reading is really the first step toward becoming an accomplished Lincoln-Douglas debater. The next step is practicing. But there are some fundamental points that bear repeating.

The affirmative issues of value term, value criterion, and value justification can be considered essential parts of an affirmative case. However, they are not necessarily voting issues. While you should try to include these issues in your case, there are no specific rules that state you must include them. However, you are likely to be more successful as an affirmative Lincoln-Douglas debater if you build your case around these stock issues and take advantage of the organizational strategies presented in this chapter.

Chapter 10

The Negative Position in Lincoln-Douglas Debate

While the affirmative is generally believed to have three stock, or essential, issues in Lincoln-Douglas debate, the negative has only one. The negative's stock issue is to attack the affirmative's value justification, the arguments the affirmative presents to support the value criterion. This is the responsibility for clash in the debate. If the negative does not clash with the affirmative's position, the affirmative can argue that the negative has not fulfilled its obligations and should lose.

Since the inception of Lincoln-Douglas debate, the negative speaker has had three options: directly refute the affirmative case; present an independent negative case; or combine refutation and a negative case. All three options are effective and work well. The combination is probably the most effective, because it creates the most work for the affirmative and gives the judge two strong reasons instead of one to vote for the negative.

No matter which option you choose, you have the basic responsibility of clash, either with the affirmative's interpretation of the topic or with the topic itself. You may directly refute the affirmative's case. The best way is by attacking all the arguments one at a time, as they were presented. Make sure to tell the judge where you are in the affirmative case by signposting. Signposting is referring directly to the affirmative's points. For example, stating, "On the affirmative's first contention of unconstitutionality..." will help the judge immediately identify what you will be arguing.

Negative Constructive

Refutation

When refuting the affirmative position, there are certain aspects of the debate that every negative speaker should consider. The first is the affirmative's definitions. You do not have to accept the affirmative value term or value criterion. You can redefine the value term. You can offer a new definition for any of the other terms in the resolution, or you can offer an entirely new value criterion. But you must make sure that your new definitions are superior to or more appropriate than the affirmative's. You can choose to accept the affirmative's definitions or value criterion, but then you are bound by the affirmative's interpretation for the remainder of the debate. If the affirmative did not give specific definitions, especially for the value criterion, you have the right to define them as you wish—providing your definitions are reasonable.

After attacking or redefining the definitions, the next step is to attack directly the affirmative's arguments, or value justification. Attacking the value justification is an essential negative strategy. If you can show successfully that the value justification does not support the value, the affirmative will have a very difficult time winning the debate.

The Negative Case

The negative case offers several interesting attack opportunities. First, the negative case can be used to directly attack the topic. If the topic is worded so that presumption is with the negative, as in "Resolved: The two-party system is detrimental to democratic ideals," then you can simply defend the present system. You might argue that the two-party system is essential to democratic ideals. If presumption is not clear, as in the topic "Resolved: Competition is of greater value than cooperation," then you can argue that cooperation is actually greater than competition.

In either circumstance, when you present a negative case you have much the same responsibilities as the affirmative. You must define your terms, establish the value criterion, and present your value justification, or the reasons why your interpretation is superior to the affirmative's. Since you are the initiator of a new argument, you have the burden of proof for your interpretation. You must present a prima facie case by supporting your assertions with evidence. It is not enough to say "The topic is not true"; instead, you must give substantial reasons why you think the topic is not true.

The second use of the negative case applies primarily to quasi-policy topics. It involves attacking the affirmative's interpretation of the topic. Because there is an implied plan in a quasi-policy topic, the negative can legitimately argue against the implied plan. The first way to do this is to examine what might happen if the affirmative value case is accepted. For example, under the topic "Resolved: Censorship of educational materials in elementary and high schools is justified," the affirmative has established the value criterion of "protection of children" as the most important value for the debate. You attempt to show the potential harms of the affirmative's case. Such an argument may be called *value implications*, because you are examining what may occur if the affirmative case is accepted. For example, you might argue two main points:

1. If children are "protected" from differing viewpoints, they will be more afraid of people and less able to take care of themselves.

2. Censorship is a violation of the First Amendment to the Constitution.

As the negative speaker, you would then explain that the value of the Constitution is more important than the value of censorship.

It is important to listen carefully to the affirmative case to hear exactly what is being advocated in terms of a value. You can prepare briefs (outlined arguments prepared ahead of time) by thinking of all the possible interpretations of the topic. You will want to be able to apply these briefs to the specific affirmative arguments.

Because experience has shown that the best negative approach is a combination of straight refutation and a negative case, negative cases generally last between three and four minutes. This allows time for straight refutation. In your presentation, it is most effective to first offer straight refutation. Then you can finish with your own case. This way you leave the judge with your interpretation of the topic, rather than with the affirmative's.

Cross-Examination

The negative speaker conducts the first cross-examination period in a Lincoln-Douglas debate. As in standard cross-examination debate, the purpose of the cross-examination is to clarify information and to probe for weaknesses. The cross-examination period is important for the negative speaker because it can provide valuable information on which to build both your arguments against the affirmative case and your negative case.

It is especially important for the negative speaker to question the value term and value justification that the affirmative has presented. For example, if you are debating the topic "Resolved: The American media do not reflect American values," the affirmative could present a case in which truth is defined as one of the most important American values. As part of the value justification, the affirmative states that news programs mostly present stories of death, destruction, and misfortune. The affirmative then states that because the American people are tired of seeing and hearing bad news, the American media do not reflect American ideals. If the affirmative reads a great deal of evidence to back up each claim, there is little sense in spending much time questioning the evidence. However, you can question the underlying or most important value, which the affirmative has defined as being truth.

During cross-examination, you might want to ask the affirmative, "Why don't the American people want to view this bad news? Is it because they are disgusted with it and no longer want to face it? Are the media presenting lies to the American people?" At this point, you may have a difficult time getting the affirmative to answer your questions. You are now exposing a fundamental weakness in the affirmative's value system. American values were defined as being predominately truth-oriented, but the value justification examples were taste- or preference-oriented. Such a conflict with a value term will make it very difficult for the affirmative to win. As blatant as this example is, it is not uncommon to find such mistakes, especially at the first tournaments of the year.

Negative Rebuttal

In Lincoln-Douglas debate, the negative speaker has only one rebuttal. Since this is your last speech, you want to be sure to respond to the affirmative attacks and also to stress what you believe to be the key issues of the debate. You should begin with the affirmative case. Use the four-step method for each argument:

1. State where you are in the debate.

2. Restate your opponent's response.

3. State your response.

4. Summarize the impact of the argument on the debate.

If there are many arguments remaining because neither you nor your opponent have dropped any, then you have a couple of strategies to choose from. If the affirmative case has many contentions and each one has three to four pieces of evidence, you may not have the time to respond to each piece of evidence. You should try instead to focus on the basic analysis behind each contention and beat that. Besides, much of the evidence may be redundant. Therefore, you can respond to the entire contention without worrying about each piece of evidence separately. Because Lincoln-Douglas debate stresses the communicative factor, your first concern should be to debate your opponent clearly and intelligibly.

If the affirmative case is very shallow or has very little detail, you may have time to respond to each separate point and piece of evidence. Remember, because you must also rebuild your own case, you should not spend more than three or four minutes of your time on the affirmative case. End with your case. At this point you will want to focus clearly on the key issues of your case. If you have time, you might try to slow down and persuasively examine why your case is superior to that of the affirmative speaker. You want to leave the judge with a favorable impression of your case and of you.

Summary

The negative speaker in Lincoln-Douglas has the responsibility for clash in the debate. As a negative, you can clash with the affirmative through straight refutation, the negative case, or a combination. Because the format of Lincoln-Douglas is different from standard debate, you may have to employ some different strategies in order to persuade the judge to vote negative. There are no set rules that specify what you must do, but you are likely to be successful if you combine value justification, value implication, and topic attacks in your constructive and rebuttal speeches.

Chapter 11

Evidence in Lincoln-Douglas Debate

E vidence plays a slightly different role in Lincoln-Douglas debate than it does in standard team debate. Since value judgments rest on subjective attitudes and opinions, the proof you use to support a Lincoln-Douglas resolution can have a much more emotional basis than the proof you use to support a policy debate resolution. However, this is not to say that you do not need carefully chosen and documented evidence for Lincoln-Douglas debate. Without evidence, your arguments may be nothing more than shallow self-interpretations of the topic.

Types of Evidence

When you research for Lincoln-Douglas debate, you may select for primary data some things that you would overlook or reject for standard debate. The three types of evidence that are most frequently used in Lincoln-Douglas debating are testimony, narrative example, and facts.

Testimony is a prime source of evidence for Lincoln-Douglas debate. It is built on source credibility and encompasses a variety of quotations. The recency of a quotation may have little relevance to its value as data. What is more important is how well regarded the source is.

Narrative example can be very useful in Lincoln-Douglas debate. Narrative example allows you to create for the judge the behavior or environment under consideration. You can encourage the judge to empathize with a set of actions and conditions.

Finally, facts are a helpful form of data. However, facts play a subsidiary role in Lincoln-Douglas debate. Empirical data should always be presented within the context of the values debated. Under the topic "Resolved: U.S. television programs do more harm than good for society," citing statistics from opinion polls about program content may further the debate. If the value being debated is "protection of children," an effective use of statistics might involve citing the number of homicides an average child is likely to witness on television.

Sources of Evidence

One of the most valuable resources for debate evidence is the *Readers' Guide to Periodical Literature.* This guide is available in nearly every library. It indexes a great number of magazine articles by subject. Another excellent source for magazine articles is a microform reader called *Text on Microform* (TOM). It contains an abridged version of the last six years of the *Readers' Guide.* It is very easy to use and is available at most college and large public libraries.

Two magazines that are sometimes overlooked are the *Congressional Digest* and *Vital Speeches of the Day.* The first offers in-depth analysis of a single issue currently being discussed in Congress. The second magazine lists important speeches from world leaders on a variety of subjects.

An important source for newspaper articles is the *Social Index Resource Service* (SIRS). It indexes newspaper articles from across the country. Often, newspaper articles go into more depth than major magazine articles do.

For some topics, magazines and newspapers will not contain the needed information. Consider this topic: "Resolved: A parliamentary system of government would better meet the underlying values of the U.S. Constitution." Much of your information will come from comparative government textbooks and specialized encyclopedias. Three such encyclopedias are the *Encyclopedia of the Social Sciences,* the *International Encyclopedia of the Social Sciences,* and *The Encyclopedia of Philosophy.* These three books offer in-depth analyses of social science and philosophical ideas that can ultimately provide a wealth of information for any value topic.

Some final words on where to find information: Browse, read a major daily newspaper, and ask your librarian for help.

Evaluating Evidence

The rules for evaluating evidence for Lincoln-Douglas debate are similar to the rules for standard team debate. The most important elements are source credibility, date, and value for the debate. Source credibility is especially important. In standard debate, a quote from *Children's World* magazine might not be as effective as a quote from a publication such as *Newsweek* or *The Wall Street Journal*. However, in Lincoln-Douglas debate, a quote from *Children's World* might have a great deal of impact for certain topics. Also, the date of publication of the quote may be less important in Lincoln-Douglas debate, since many debate topics are philosophical and historical in nature.

As in standard debate, it is important to evaluate the value of the specific evidence. In debating a topic like "Resolved: Modern art is superior to ancient Egyptian art," a quote such as "Modern art is fun" carries less weight than "The number of museums displaying only modern art has tripled since 1978 and modern art museums have grossed more than three hundred million dollars during that same time."

Organizing Evidence

After you have researched your topic, you will need to organize your evidence. As in other forms of debate, you should be able to locate any piece of evidence quickly during a debate.

The first step is to type each piece of evidence on an index card. You may choose to photocopy the material and paste it onto a card. The important consideration is that your evidence cards must be easy to read. You should include a full citation on each card, listing the author, title of the book or magazine, page, date, and any other pertinent information for locating your source. You also may want to include a short list of the author's qualifications. For example, if the evidence cited is published in *Juvenile Behavior and Delinquency*, you may wish to note that the author is director of delinquency studies at a major university. (You would also note the university.)

Once you have amassed a body of evidence cards, you will need to arrange them for easy reference. The first division to make is between affirmative and negative evidence. In Lincoln-Douglas debate, you will be expected to debate both sides of each topic. After separating affirmative and negative cards, the divisions will become more specific. For example, if the topic is "Resolved: Censorship of educational material is justified," you may have divisions under the affirmative heading for "Harmful Material," "Parental Rights," and "Current Laws." Under each of these headings, you may create sub-headings. For "Harmful Material" your sub-headings might include:

Harmful Material
1. Sex education
    a. religious
    b. philosophical
2. Literature
3. Audio-visual

Under each heading and sub-heading, you will file cards dealing with that specific idea. You may find that some cards will fit under two headings. You also may find that you need a heading for only one card. It is better to have duplicate cards and small categories than to have an incomplete set of evidence or such broad categories that you are unable to find anything.

Summary

As in other forms of debate, you are responsible for gathering, evaluating, and organizing evidence for Lincoln-Douglas debate. Because Lincoln-Douglas debate involves value propositions, however, you may be able to use some forms of evidence that you would not use in standard debate. The credibility of your sources may be much more important than the recency of the data.

Chapter 12

Strategies for Success in Lincoln-Douglas Debate

I n team debate, you are primarily concerned with the logical aspect of persuasion. In Lincoln-Douglas, you must balance the logic of your arguments with your ethos or credibility. This credibility is established by the manner in which you present your message, in other words, your style. It is important to remember that you are presenting your case before another human being—the judge. Understanding something about the various types of judges enables you to use your debating style successfully from tournament to tournament.

Judges

The more you compete, the more adept you will become at understanding particular judges. Generally, you will encounter three types of judges: community or parent judges, college judges, and coach judges.

Community or parent judges are common at smaller, more local tournaments. Although they are genuinely conscientious, they may not be as well versed in debate theory as you are. Because of this, they may not be able to flow quickly or be familiar with the intricacies of the specific topic. Be careful to avoid any jargon, either debate- or topic-oriented. "LDCs" may mean "lesser-developed countries" to you, but the expression may mean nothing to a community judge.

It is also very important that you be well organized in your presentation. You should always signpost your arguments. The judge may not be taking notes and probably will not remember what Contention 1, Subpoint 3 refers to unless you remind him or her.

College judges are generally quite skilled in public speaking and may be members of college forensic teams. If so, they may flow whatever you tell them. Therefore, you should be prepared for a faster round if you are attending a tournament with college judges. They may even have a background in debate theory and therefore be better able to follow a highly technical debate than a community judge. Do not think, though, that the judge will just take notes and figure everything out. You have the ultimate responsibility for insuring that the judge understands all of the arguments as well as why your arguments are superior.

Debate coach judges are certainly well aware of the topic, as well as the arguments and perhaps even the evidence. Often, at large tournaments, coaches are required to judge. As long as you are clear in your analysis and you adapt to whether the coach is flow or nonflow, you should be able to impress even the most particular of judges.

Style

Your style depends on both your verbal and nonverbal presentation. Verbal presentation includes rate of delivery, vocal variety, and courtesy. Nonverbal presentation includes eye contact, body control, and gesture. The more you work to control all of these elements, the more effective your debate style will be, and the more confident you will become.

Rate of Delivery

Much has been written about speed in debate. Recently, team debaters at a national tournament were clocked at an average of 400 words per minute. Compare this to normal conversation speed, which is 125 to 150 words per minute. You can easily see the difference!

Rate of delivery was one of the reasons for the formation of Lincoln-Douglas debate. Initially, the acceptable rate of delivery in Lincoln-Douglas was quite slow. Over the past several years, however, speed has increased in Lincoln-Douglas debate. This does not mean that the rate of delivery common to standard debate is accepted in Lincoln-Douglas tournaments. In fact, there does not seem to be a consistent rule among judges or between tournaments. The best advice is to speak so as to best communicate. It is your responsibility to insure that you are understood. This most likely means speaking at a rate that is comfortable for you and the judge.

Vocal Variety

We have all heard monotone speakers. No matter what is being said, the emphasis is the same. Vocal variety involves rate, pitch, and emphasis. Studying these elements can help you become a more effective communicator, and thus a better debater.

The first of these characteristics, rate, has already been discussed. But simply avoiding speaking too rapidly is not all that is involved in rate. Think about how you deliver messages in normal conversation. You slow your rate of delivery when you are trying to make a serious point or indicate your own thoughtfulness. You may speed up when you are excited or are covering common information. Varying your rate of delivery is a fairly easy way to improve your effectiveness as a communicator.

Pitch, however, can be a more elusive vocal characteristic to master. Pitch, high or low, refers to your natural, comfortable vocal range. You should not try to change your vocal range because you may harm your vocal cords. However, you can use your full pitch. In normal conversation, many people use less than eight different notes of their total vocal range. Vocal range is an important aspect of Lincoln-Douglas delivery. A narrow pitch range often communicates boredom or lack of caring.

An extremely wide pitch range can communicate artificiality or uncontrolled fear. Generally, let the situation and the message dictate your pitch range. In normal conversation, a higher pitch often suggests excitement and a lower pitch seriousness, questions end on a higher pitch, and pitch changes with differences in meaning.

Another reason to use your full pitch range is the physical distances involved in debate rounds. While you are at the front of the room debating, your judge will usually be in the back. In order for the judge to hear your message clearly, you might have to exaggerate your normal range. Of course, debating in a small room means that you may need to lower your pitch and, especially, your volume.

The last quality of vocal variety, emphasis, is more word-specific. Emphasis is the use of loudness, pitch, or rate to make certain words or phrases stand out. In a debate on gun control, there could be many ways of reading the sentence "Gun control does not decrease murders." Notice how different meanings may be achieved by emphasizing different words:

1. **Gun control** does not decrease murders. (Emphasizes the policy of gun control as opposed to some other policy.)

2. Gun control does **not** decrease murders. (States that there is no link between gun control and murders.)

3. Gun control does not decrease **murders.** (Suggests that murders are not decreased, but perhaps some other crimes are decreased.)

Practicing vocal variety is important because it can increase the judge's understanding and your own credibility as a speaker.

Courtesy

Very few people intend to be rude to their opponents, but many debaters appear to be just that. The pressure of competition can make even the most sincere and courteous person appear to be rude or belligerent. Perhaps the most difficult time of the debate is the cross-examination. During this period, you are grilled about the finer points of your case. It is therefore more important than at any other time during the debate to make an extra effort to be cordial.

The first guideline is not to ask any questions of your examiner unless you truly did not understand the examiner's question. Second, try to give the shortest yet most complete answer possible. Do not admit that your case has some glaring weaknesses, but do not try to deliberately waste your opponent's time. Your opponent may direct you to answer with only a yes or no response. You should do your best to comply, but do not sell yourself short. Some questions require more than a yes or no answer. Such responses, when necessary, generally are not considered rude. However, if your opponent does not want you to answer with a lengthy statement, then you may need to hold your temper in check, smile at the judge, and answer as accurately as possible. If you are answering as well as you can and your opponent is still harrassing you, then chances are your judge will notice this and may make a comment about it on the ballot.

When asking questions, you want to give your opponent a reasonable opportunity for defense. However, you do not want to allow him or her to monopolize your time. You may interrupt your opponent to ask another question or to redirect the line of answering. Just be careful not to intentionally antagonize or purposely forbid your opponent a chance to answer.

Eye Contact

Eye contact is an important consideration in debate. You must establish eye contact with your opponent and with the judge. Many coaches believe that you should never look directly at your opponent during cross-examination. By looking only at the judge, you set up an emotional superiority over your opponent. Certainly, by ignoring your opponent you do create a barrier or distance, but by ignoring him or her you also may appear a bit ridiculous. Not only is it difficult to completely avoid eye contact during cross-examination, it is also unnatural.

This is not to say that you should look only at your opponent during cross-examination. The majority of your eye contact should be with the judge. The judge is the one who makes the decision. Most speech texts acknowledge that eye contact is one of the more important characteristics of building credibility. However, an occasional glance at your opponent, especially when you are asking a particularly poignant question or giving a well-detailed answer, will not detract from your credibility and may in fact be quite beneficial. In a recent poll conducted of community judges in California, eye contact, both with the judge and with the opponent, was found to be important.

After several cross-examination practice sessions, you will develop a style that is comfortable for you and reasonable for the judge. Above all, Lincoln-Douglas is designed to help you become a better communicator. If you are not comfortable with your presentation, then chances are that neither is the judge.

Body Control

Body control refers to such things as pacing about and using the podium. Many people develop nervous habits while speaking. They may not even be aware of these habits, although they are often glaringly obvious to the judge. Pacing is unpurposefully walking back and forth while speaking. The key to understanding pacing is that it is unpurposeful. Walking or taking a step while making a new point can be helpful to the audience, but pacing is not.

Another nervous habit is gripping the podium. Some speakers grab the podium so tightly that it appears nothing short of a tornado could knock them loose. The podium can become a crutch if not used properly. To use a podium properly, you must first consider your body type. If you are short, a podium may block you from the judge—not only physically (the judge may be able to see only your head and shoulders) but also psychologically. A speaker who always stands behind a podium or lectern may seem to be hiding. There is little chance for any audience involvement. In Lincoln-Douglas debate, you are trying to convince the judge that your interpretation of the topic is superior to your opponent's. You want the judge to feel comfortable with your case as well as with you.

Gesture

The last aspect of nonverbal communication is gesture. Gestures are purposeful uses of the hands, face, or any other part of the body. Nervously playing with your pen is not a gesture because it is not purposeful. Instead, it is a distraction. Shrugging your shoulders to show confusion and pounding your fist to show anger are common gestures. When giving a speech you may become nervous and self-conscious. You may think that any gestures you use look stupid or distracting. Quite often, just the opposite is true. Your judge often will be in the back of the room. He or she may not be able to see all of your gestures, especially if they are small. This means that instead of using few or small gestures, you should actually exaggerate them just a bit.

Summary

Successful Lincoln-Douglas debaters work to improve their credibility with judges. One way to do this is to know the different types of judges, and to tailor your presentation to meet the judge's needs. Another way is to develop a personal debating style that is comfortable for you and pleasing to the judge. You should be in control of both the verbal and nonverbal aspects of your presentation. Rate of delivery, vocal variety, a courteous manner, eye contact, body control, and use of gesture all combine to impress a judge. As you develop your style, you will also develop greater self-confidence as a debater.

NTC DEBATE AND SPEECH BOOKS

Debate
ADVANCED DEBATE, ed. Thomas & Hart
BASIC DEBATE, Fryar, Thomas, & Goodnight
COACHING AND DIRECTING FORENSICS, Klopf
CROSS-EXAMINATION IN DEBATE, Copeland
DICTIONARY OF DEBATE, Hanson
FORENSIC TOURNAMENTS: PLANNING AND ADMINISTRATION, Goodnight & Zarefsky
GETTING STARTED IN DEBATE, Goodnight
JUDGING ACADEMIC DEBATE, Ulrich
MODERN DEBATE CASE TECHNIQUES, Terry et al.
MOVING FROM POLICY TO VALUE DEBATE, Richards
STRATEGIC DEBATE, Wood & Goodnight
STUDENT CONGRESS & LINCOLN-DOUGLAS DEBATE, Giertz & Mezzera

Speech Communication
ACTIVITIES FOR EFFECTIVE COMMUNICATION, LiSacchi
THE BASICS OF SPEECH, Galvin, Cooper, & Gordon
CONTEMPORARY SPEECH, HopKins & Whitaker
CREATIVE SPEAKING, Buys et al.
DYNAMICS OF SPEECH, Myers & Herndon
GETTING STARTED IN PUBLIC SPEAKING, Prentice & Payne
LISTENING BY DOING, Galvin
LITERATURE ALIVE! Gamble & Gamble
MEETINGS: RULES & PROCEDURES, Pohl
PERSON TO PERSON, Galvin & Book
PUBLIC SPEAKING TODAY! Prentice & Payne
SELF-AWARENESS, Ratliffe & Herman
SPEAKING BY DOING, Buys, Sill, & Beck

For a current catalog and information about our complete line
of language arts books, write:
National Textbook Company,
a division of NTC Publishing Group
4255 West Touhy Avenue
Lincolnwood (Chicago), Illinois 60646-1975 U.S.A.